National Parks
and Conservation Association

Thomas C. Kiernan
President

Dear Reader:

Welcome to the National Parks and Conservation Association's national park guidebooks—a series designed to help you to discover America's most significant scenery, history, and culture found in the more than 370 areas that make up the U.S. National Park System.

The park system represents the best America has to offer for our natural, historical, and cultural heritage—a collection of resources that we have promised to preserve "unimpaired" for future generations. We hope that, in addition to giving you practical information to help you plan your visits to national park areas, these guides also will help you be a more aware, more responsible visitor to our parks. The cautions offered at the beginning of these guides are not to frighten you away but to remind you that we all have a role in protecting the parks. For it is only if each and every one of us takes responsibility that these special places will be preserved and available for future generations to enjoy.

For more than three-quarters of a century, the National Parks and Conservation Association has been America's leading citizen advocacy group working solely to protect the national parks. Whether fighting to preserve the wilderness character of Cumberland Island National Seashore, preventing the expansion of a major airport outside the Everglades, stopping a coal mine at Cumberland Gap, or defeating legislation that could lead to the closure of many national parks, NPCA has made the voices of its members and supporters heard in efforts to protect the resources of our national parks from harm.

We hope that you will join in our commitment. Remember: when you visit the parks, take only pictures, and leave only footprints.

1776 Massachusetts Avenue, N.W., Washington, D.C. 20036-1904
Telephone (202) 223-NPCA(6722) • Fax (202) 659-0650

♻ PRINTED ON RECYCLED PAPER

CONTENTS

▲ Bighorn sheep in Glacier National Park, Montana

Pacific Northwest Region

San Juan
Island
NHP

Ross
Lake
NRA

North Cascades NP

Lake Chelan NRA

Glacier N

Klondike
Gold Rush
NHP
Seattle

Coulee
Dam NRA

Olympic NP

PACIFIC

OCEAN

Ebey's
Landing
NH RES

Roosevelt
Lake

*Lake
Chelan*

Spokane

WASHINGTON

Columbia

Mount Rainier NP

Clark

Fork

Snake

Nez Perce NHP

Fort Clatsop
N MEM

Whitman
Mission NHS

Lochsa

Fort Vancouver
NHS

Columbia

Selway

Portland

Salmon

Salem

Snake

John Day
Fossil Beds
NM

IDA

OREGON

Boise

Snake

of the

Crater Lake
NP

Oregon
Caves NM

Ouyhee

Hagerman
Fossil Beds NM

*Upper
Klamath Lake*

City of

N

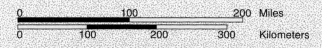

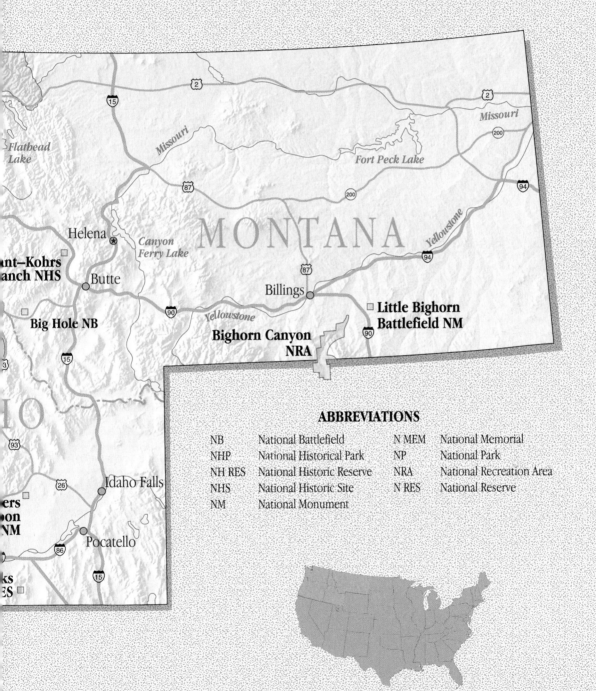

MONTANA

Flathead Lake

Missouri

Missouri

Fort Peck Lake

Canyon Ferry Lake

Yellowstone

Helena

Butte

Billings

Little Bighorn
Battlefield NM

nt–Kohrs
anch NHS

Big Hole NB

Bighorn Canyon
NRA

IDAHO

Idaho Falls

Pocatello

ABBREVIATIONS

NB	National Battlefield	N MEM	National Memorial
NHP	National Historical Park	NP	National Park
NH RES	National Historic Reserve	NRA	National Recreation Area
NHS	National Historic Site	N RES	National Reserve
NM	National Monument		

General Information

▲ *Wildflowers at the Craters of the Moon National Monument, Idaho*

GENERAL INFORMATION

Whether you're an American history buff or a birdwatcher, a lover of rocky coastlines or marshy swamps, a dedicated environmentalist or a weekend rambler, and whether you're seeking a way to spend a carefully planned month-long vacation or an unexpectedly free sunny afternoon—the national parks are for you. They offer a broad spectrum of natural and cultural resources in all 50 states as well as Guam, Puerto Rico, the Virgin Islands, and American Samoa where you can learn, exercise, participate in activities, and be constantly moved and inspired by the riches available. Perhaps most important of all, as one of the National Park System's 280 million annual visitors, you become part of the attempt to preserve our natural and historical treasures for present and future generations.

This guidebook will help you do that, as one in a series of eight Regional National Park Guides covering all the units in the National Park System. This section of general information provides both an overview of key facts that can be applied to every unit and a brief history of the National Parks and Conservation Association (NPCA).

SPECIAL PARK PASSES

Some parks charge entrance fees to help offset their operational costs. Several options for special entrance passes are available, enabling you to choose the most appropriate and economical way for you and your family and friends to visit sites.

Park Pass: For this annual entrance permit to a specific fee-charging park, monument, historic site, or recreation area in the National Park System, the cost is usually $10 or $15 depending on the area. Such a pass does not cover any fees other than entrance for the permit holder and any accompanying passengers in a private noncommercial vehicle or, in the case of walk-in facilities, the permit holder's spouse, children, and parents. The pass may be purchased in person or by mail from the unit at which it will be used. It is nontransferable and nonrefundable.

Golden Eagle Passport: This annual entrance pass admits visitors to all the federal lands that charge entrance fees; these include national parks, monuments, historic sites, recreation areas, national forests, and national wildlife refuges. The pass costs $50 and is valid for one year from purchase. It does not cover any fees other than entrance for the permit holder and any accompanying passengers in a private noncommercial vehicle or, in the case of walk-in facilities, the holder's spouse, children, and parents. The Golden Eagle Passport may be purchased in person or by mail from the National Park Service, Office of Public Inquiries, Room 1013, U.S. Department of the Interior, 18th & C Streets, N.W., Washington, DC 20240 (202-208-4747) or at any of the seven National Park Service (NPS) field offices, any of the nine U.S. Forest Service regional offices, or any national park unit and other federal areas that charge an entrance fee. It is nontransferable and nonrefundable.

Golden Age Passport: A one-time $10 fee for this pass allows lifetime entrance to all federal fee-charging areas as described in the Golden Eagle Passport section for citizens and permanent residents of the United States who are 62 years of age or older and any accompanying passengers in a private noncommercial vehicle or, in the case of walk-in facilities, the holder's spouse and children. This pass also entitles the holder to a 50 percent discount on use fees charged in park areas. The Golden Age Passport must be obtained IN PERSON at any of the locations listed in the Golden Eagle Passport section; mail requests are not accepted. Applicants must provide proof of age, such as a driver's license or birth certificate, or sign an affidavit attesting to eligibility.

Golden Access Passport: This free lifetime entrance permit to all federal fee-charging areas as described in the Golden Eagle Passport section is available for citizens and permanent residents of the United States who are visually impaired or permanently disabled and any accompanying passengers in a private noncommercial vehicle or, in the case of walk-in facilities, the permit holder's spouse, children, and parents. It also entitles the holder to a 50 percent discount on use fees charged in park areas. The Golden Access Passport must be obtained IN PERSON at any of the locations listed in the Golden Eagle Passport section; mail requests are not accepted. Applicant must provide proof of eligibility to receive federal benefits or sign an affidavit attesting to one's eligibility.

PASSPORT TO YOUR NATIONAL PARKS

The *Passport to Your National Parks* is a special commemorative item designed to serve as a companion for park visitors. This informative and unique publication records each visit through special regional and national stamps and cancellations. When you visit any national park, be sure to have your Passport canceled with a rubber stamp marking the name of the park and the date you were there. The passport gives you the opportunity to share and relive your journey through America's national parks and will become a travel record to cherish for years. Passports cost $4.95; a full set of ten national and regional stamps are $3.95. The national parks represented in the stamp set vary from year to year. For ordering information, call 800-821-2903, or write to Eastern National Park & Monument Association, 110 Hector Street, Suite 105, Conshohocken, PA 19428.

HELPFUL TRIP-PLANNING PUBLICATIONS

Two volumes offer descriptive text on the National Park System: *Exploring Our National Parks and Monuments,* by Devereux Butcher (ninth edition by Russell D. Butcher), and *Exploring Our National Historic Parks and Sites,* by Russell D. Butcher. These books feature descriptions and black-and-white photographs of more than 370 National Park System units. Both volumes also contain chapters on possible new parks, threats to the parks, a history of NPCA, and the national park standards. To order, contact Roberts

Rinehart Publishers, 6309 Monarch Park Place, Niwot, CO 80503; 800-352-1985 or 303-530-4400.

NPCA offers the following brochures at no charge: *The National Parks: How to Have a Quality Experience* and *Visiting Battlefields: The Civil War.* These brochures provide helpful information on how best to enjoy a visit to the national parks. NPCA members can also receive the *Park System Map and Guide, The National Parks Index, The National Parks Camping Guide,* and *Lesser Known Areas* as part of NPCA's PARK-PAK by calling 202-223-6722, ext. 214.

The Story Behind the Scenery® and *The Continuing Story®* series are lavishly illustrated books providing informative text and magnificent photographs of the landscapes, flora, and fauna of our national parklands. More than 100 titles on the national parks, historic events, and Indian cultures, as well as an annual national parks calendar, are available. For information, call toll free 800-626-9673, fax to 702-731-9421, or write to KC Publications, 3245 E. Patrick Lane, Suite A, Las Vegas, NV 89120.

The National Parks: Index and *Lesser Known Areas,* both produced by the National Park Service, can be ordered by contacting the Superintendent of Documents, U.S. Government Printing Office, Washington, DC 20402-9325; 202-512-1800. To receive at no charge the *National Park System Map and Guide,* the *National Trails System Map and Guide;* or an *Official Map and Guide* of specific national parks, contact National Park Service, Office of Information, P.O. Box 37127, Washington, DC 20013-7127; 202-208-4747.

National Parks Visitor Facilities and Services is a directory of vendors authorized to serve park visitors through contracts with the National Park Service. Concessionaires offering lodging, food, beverages, outfitting, tours, trail rides, and other activities and services are listed alphabetically. To order, contact the National Park Hospitality Association, 1331 Pennsylvania Avenue, N.W., Suite 724, Washington, DC 20004; 202-662-7097.

Great Walks, Inc., publishes six pocket-sized books of detailed information on specific trails in Yosemite; Sequoia and Kings Canyon in California; Big Bend; Great Smoky Mountains; and Acadia and Mount Desert Island in Maine. For information, send $1 (refundable with your first order) to Great Walks, P.O. Box 410, Goffstown, NH 03045.

The U.S. Bureau of Land Management (BLM) offers free maps that detail recreation areas and scenic and backcountry roads and trails.

These are available by contacting the BLM at the Department of the Interior, 1849 C St., N.W., Suite 5600, Washington, DC 20240; 202-452-5125. In addition, *Beyond the National Parks: A Recreational Guide to Public Lands in the West,* published by the Smithsonian Institution Press, is an informative guidebook to many special places administered by the BLM. *America's Secret Recreation Areas,* by Michael Hodgson, is an excellent resource for little-known natural areas in 12 Western states. It details 270

▲ *Coulee Dam, Lake Roosevelt National Recreation Area, Washington*

million acres of land administered by BLM, with campgrounds, recreational activities, trails, maps, facilities, and much more. The 1995-96 edition is published by Foghorn Press and is available for $17.95 by calling 800-FOGHORN.

The National Wildlife Refuge Visitors Guide can be ordered free from the U.S. Fish and Wildlife Service's Publications Unit at 4401 North Fairfax Drive, MS 130 Webb, Arlington, VA 22203; 703-358-1711.

The four-volume *Birds of the National Parks* by Roland H. Wauer, a retired NPS interpreter and biologist, provides an excellent reference on the parks' birds and their seasons and habitats. This series, written for the average rather than specialist park visitor, is unfortunately out of print.

SAFETY AND REGULATIONS

To protect the national parks' natural and cultural resources and the millions of people who come to enjoy them, the National Park Service asks every visitor to abide by some important regulations. Park staffs do all they can to help you have a safe and pleasant visit, but your cooperation is essential.

Some park hazards—deep lakes, sheer cliffs, extremely hot or cold temperatures—cannot be eliminated. However, accidents and illnesses can be prevented if you use the same common sense you would at home and become familiar with the park. Take some time before your trip or when you first arrive to get to know the park's regulations, warnings, and potential hazards. If you have children, make sure they understand such precautions, and keep a careful watch over them, especially in potentially dangerous situations. If you are injured or become ill, the staff can help by directing you to the nearest medical center and, in some parks, by giving you emergency care.

A few rules and safety tips are common to many parks. At all parks, you must keep your campsite clean and the park free of litter by disposing of refuse in trash receptacles. The National Park Service also asks you to follow federal regulations and refrain from the abuse of alcohol and the use of drugs, which are often contributing factors to injuries and deaths. Other rules and safety tips are outlined in the "Special Advisories and Visitor Ethics" section; more detailed information may be provided in park brochures, on signs, and on bulletin boards at camping areas and other park sites. The National Park Service asks that you report any violation of park regulations to park authorities. If you have any questions, seek the advice of a ranger.

SPECIAL ADVISORIES AND VISITOR ETHICS

Safe Driving

Park roads are designed for sightseeing, not speeding. Because roads are often narrow and winding and sometimes steep, visitors should drive carefully, observe posted speed limits, and be alert for wildlife, pedestrians, bicyclists, other drivers, fallen rocks or trees, slippery roads, and other hazards. Be especially alert for motorists who might stop unexpectedly for sightseeing or wildlife viewing. Visitors are urged to use roadside pullouts instead of stopping on the roadway.

Campfires

Most parks permit fires, as long as certain rules are followed. To avoid a wildfire that would be dangerous to people, property, and natural resources, parks may allow only certain types of campfires—fires only in grills provided, for example, or in designated fire rings. Firewood gathering may be prohibited or restricted to certain areas, so visitors should plan on bringing their own fuel supply. Fires should be kept under control, should never be left unattended, and should be thoroughly extinguished before departure.

Quiet Hours

Out of respect for other visitors, campers should keep noise to a minimum at all times, especially from 10 p.m. to 6 a.m.

Pets

Pets must always be leashed or otherwise physically restrained for the protection of the animal, other visitors, and wildlife. Pets may be prohibited from certain areas, including public buildings, trails, and the backcountry. A few parks prohibit pets altogether. Dog owners are responsible for keeping their pets quiet in camping areas and elsewhere. Guide dogs are exempted from park restrictions. Some parks provide kennel services; contact the park visitor center for information.

Protection of Valuables

Theft is just as much a problem in the national parks as elsewhere, so when leaving a campsite or heading out on a trail, visitors should take valuables along or hide them out of sight in a locked vehicle, preferably in the trunk.

Heat, Cold, and Other Hazards

Visitors should take precautions to deal with the demands and hazards of a park environment.

On hot days, pace yourself, schedule strenuous activities for the morning and evening hours, and drink plenty of water and other fluids. On cold days or if you get cold and wet, frostbite and the life-threatening illness called hypothermia can occur, so avoid subjecting yourself to these conditions for long periods. In the thinner air of mountains and high plateaus, even those tasks easy to perform at home can leave one short of breath and dizzy; the best advice is to slow down. If a thunderstorm occurs, avoid exposed areas and open bodies of water, where lightning often strikes, and keep out of low-lying areas and stream beds, where flash floods are most likely to occur.

Wild Plants and Animals

It is the responsibility of every visitor to help preserve the native plants and animals protected in the parks: leave them as you find them, undisturbed and safe. Hunting or carrying a loaded weapon is prohibited in all national parks and national monuments. Hunting during the designated season is allowed in parts of only a few National Park System areas, such as national recreation areas, national preserves, and national seashores and lakeshores. Although biting insects or toxic plants, such as poison ivy or poison oak, are the most likely danger you will encounter, visitors should be aware of hazards posed by other wild plants and animals. Rattlesnakes, ticks, and animals carrying rabies or other transmittable diseases, for instance, inhabit some parks. Any wild creature—whether it is as large as a bison or moose or as small as a raccoon or prairie dog—is unpredictable and should be viewed from a distance. Remember that feeding any wild animal is absolutely prohibited.

Campers should especially guard against attracting bears to their campsites, as a close encounter with a grizzly, brown, or black bear can result in serious injury or death. Park officials in bear country recommend, and often require, that campers take certain precautions. One is to keep a campsite clean. Bears' sensitive noses can easily detect food left on cans, bottles, and utensils or even personal items with food-like odors (toothpaste, deodorant, etc.). Second, food items should be stored in containers provided by the parks or in your vehicle, preferably out of sight in the trunk.

Bears, especially those in Yosemite, are adept at breaking into cars and other motor vehicles containing even small amounts of food and can cause extensive damage to motor vehicles as they attempt to reach what they can smell. Third, in the backcountry, food should be hung from poles or wires that are provided or from a tree; visitors should inquire at the park as to the recommended placement. In treeless surroundings, campers should store food at least 50 yards from any campsite. If bears inhabit a park on your itinerary, ask the National Park Service for a bear brochure with helpful tips on avoiding trouble in bear country and inquire if bears are a problem where you plan to hike or camp.

Backcountry Camping

Camping in the remote backcountry of a park requires much more preparation than other camping. Most parks require that you pick up a backcountry permit before your trip so that rangers will know about your plans. They can also advise you of hazards and regulations and give you up-to-date information on road, trail, river, lake, or sea conditions, weather forecasts, special fire regulations, availability of water, and other matters. Backcountry permits are available at visitor centers, headquarters, and ranger stations.

There are some basic rules to follow whenever you camp in the backcountry: stay on the trails; pack out all trash; obey fire regulations; be prepared for sudden and drastic weather changes; carry a topographic map or nautical chart when necessary; and carry plenty of food and water. In parks where water is either unavailable or scarce, you may need to carry as much as one gallon of water per person per day. In other parks, springs, streams, or lakes may be abundant, but always purify water before drinking it. Untreated water can carry contaminants. One of the most common, especially in Western parks, is *giardia*, an organism that causes an unpleasant intestinal illness. Water may have to be boiled or purified with tablets; check with the park staff for the most effective treatment.

Sanitation

Visitors should bury human waste six to eight inches below ground and a minimum of 100

feet from a watercourse. Waste water should be disposed of at least 100 feet from a watercourse or campsite. Do not wash yourself, your clothing, or your dishes in any watercourse.

CAMPING RESERVATIONS

Most campsites are available on a first-come, first-served basis, but many sites can be reserved through the National Park Reservation Service. For reservations at Acadia, Assateague Island, Cape Hatteras, Channel Islands, Chickasaw, Death Valley, Everglades, Glacier, Grand Canyon, Great Smoky Mountains, Greenbelt, Gulf Islands, Joshua Tree, Katmai, Mount Rainier, Rocky Mountain, Sequoia-Kings Canyon, Sleeping Bear Dunes, Shenandoah, Whiskeytown, and Zion, call 800-365-CAMP. For reservations for Yosemite National Park, call 800-436-PARK. Reservations can also be made at any of these parks in person. Currently, reservations can be made as much as eight weeks in advance or up to the day before the start of a camping stay. Please have credit card and detailed camping information available when you call in order to facilitate the reservation process.

BIOSPHERE RESERVES AND WORLD HERITAGE SITES

A number of the national park units have received international recognition by the United Nations Educational, Scientific and Cultural Organization for their superlative natural and/or cultural values. Biosphere Reserves are representative examples of diverse natural landscapes, with both a fully protected natural core or park unit and surrounding land being managed to meet human needs. World Heritage Sites include natural and cultural sites with "universal" values that illustrate significant geological processes, may be crucial to the survival of threatened plants and animals, or demonstrate outstanding human achievement.

◀ *Craters of the Moon National Monument, Idaho*

CHECKLIST FOR HIKING AND CAMPING

Clothing

Rain gear (jacket and pants)
Windbreaker
Parka
Thermal underwear
T-shirt
Long pants and shorts
Extra wool shirt and/or sweater
Hat with brim
Hiking boots
Camp shoes/sneakers
Wool mittens
Lightweight shoes

Equipment

First-aid kit
Pocket knife
Sunglasses
Sunscreen
Topographic map
Compass
Flashlight, fresh batteries, spare bulb
Extra food and water (even for short hikes)
Waterproof matches

Fire starter
Candles
Toilet paper
Digging tool for toilet needs
Day backpack
Sleeping bag
Sleeping pad or air mattress
Tarp/ground sheet
Sturdy tent, preferably free-standing
Insect repellent
Lip balm
Pump-type water filter/water purification tablets
Water containers
Plastic trash bags
Biodegradable soap
Small towel
Toothbrush
Lightweight backpack stove/extra fuel
Cooking pot(s)
Eating utensils
Can opener
Electrolyte replacement for plain water (e.g., Gatorade)
Camera, film, lenses, filters
Binoculars
Sewing kit
Lantern
Nylon cord (50 feet)
Whistle
Signal mirror

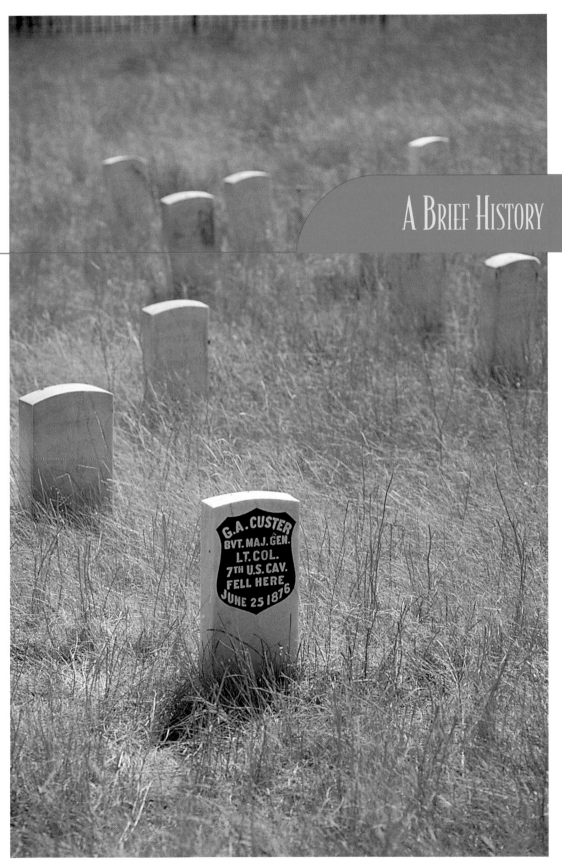

A Brief History

▲ Custer's grave at Little Bighorn Battlefield National Monument, Montana

A Brief History of the National Parks and Conservation Association

In 1916, when Congress established the National Park Service to administer the then nearly 40 national parks and monuments, the agency's first director, Stephen Tyng Mather, quickly saw the need for a private organization, independent of the federal government, to be the citizens' advocate for the parks.

Consequently, on May 19, 1919, the National Parks Association—later renamed the National Parks and Conservation Association (NPCA)—was founded in Washington, D.C. The National Park Service's former public relations director, Robert Sterling Yard, was named to lead the new organization—a position he held for a quarter century.

The association's chief objectives were then and continue to be the following: to vigorously oppose threats to the integrity of the parks; to advocate worthy and consistent standards of *national* significance for the addition of new units to the National Park System; and, through a variety of educational means, to promote the public understanding and appreciation of the parks. From the beginning, threats to the parks have been a major focus of the organization. One of the biggest conservation battles of NPCA's earliest years erupted in 1920, when Montana irrigation interests advocated building a dam and raising the level of Yellowstone Lake in Yellowstone National Park. Fortunately, this threat to the world's first national park was ultimately defeated—the first landmark victory of the fledgling citizens' advocacy group on behalf of the national parks.

At about the same time, a controversy developed over the authority given to the Water Power Commission (later renamed the Federal Power Commission) to authorize the construction of hydropower projects in national parks. The commission had already approved the flooding of Hetch Hetchy Valley in Yosemite National Park. In the ensuing political struggle, NPCA pushed for an amendment to the water power law that would prohibit such projects in all national parks. A compromise produced only a partial victory: the ban applied to the parks then in existence, but not to parks yet to be established. As a result, each new park's enabling legislation would have to expressly stipulate that the park was exempt from the commission's authority to develop hydropower projects. Yet this success, even if partial, was significant.

Also in the 1920s, NPCA successfully urged establishment of new national parks: Shenandoah, Great Smoky Mountains, Carlsbad Caverns, Bryce Canyon, and a park that later became Kings Canyon, as well as an expanded Sequoia. The association also pushed to expand Yellowstone, Grand Canyon, and Rocky Mountain national parks, pointing out that "the boundaries of the older parks were often established arbitrarily, following ruler lines drawn in far-away offices." The association continues to advocate topographically and ecologically oriented boundary improvements for many parks.

In 1930, the establishment of Colonial National Historical Park and the George Washington Birthplace National Monument signaled a broadening of the National Park System to places of primarily historical rather than environmental importance. A number of other historical areas, such as Civil War battlefields, were soon transferred from U.S. military jurisdiction to the National Park Service, and NPCA accurately predicted that this new category of parks "will rapidly surpass, in the number of units, its world-celebrated scenic" parks. Today, there are roughly 200 historical parks out of the total of 378 units. NPCA also pushed to add other units, including Everglades National Park, which was finally established in 1947.

A new category of National Park System units was initiated with the establishment of Cape Hatteras National Seashore in North Carolina. However, in spite of NPCA opposition, Congress permitted public hunting in the seashore—a precedent that subsequently opened the way to allow this consumptive resource use in other national seashores, national lakeshores, national rivers, and national preserves. With the exception of traditional, subsistence hunting in Alaska national preserves, NPCA continues to oppose hunting in all national parks and monuments.

In contrast to its loss at Cape Hatteras, NPCA achieved a victory regarding Kings Canyon National Park as a result of patience and tenacity. When the park was established in 1940, two valleys—Tehipite and Cedar Grove—were left out of the park as a concession to hydroelectric power and irrigation interests. A few years later, however, as the result of concerted efforts by the association and other environmental groups, these magnificently scenic valleys were added to the park.

In 1942, the association took a major step in its public education mission when it began publishing *National Parks*. This award-winning, full-color magazine contains news, editorials, and feature articles that help to inform members about the parks, threats facing them, and opportunities for worthy new parks and offers readers a chance to participate in the protection and enhancement of the National Park System.

In one of the most heavily publicized park-protection battles of the 1950s, NPCA and other groups succeeded in blocking construction of two hydroelectric power dams that would have inundated the spectacularly scenic river canyons in Dinosaur National Monument. In the 1960s, an even bigger battle erupted over U.S. Bureau of Reclamation plans to build two dams in the Grand Canyon. But with the cooperative efforts of a number of leading environmental organizations and tremendous help from the news media, these schemes were defeated, and Grand Canyon National Park was expanded.

In 1980, the National Park System nearly tripled in size with the passage of the Alaska National Interest Lands Conservation Act (ANILCA). One of the great milestones in the history of American land conservation, ANILCA established ten new, and expanded three existing, national park units in Alaska. This carefully crafted compromise also recognized the special circumstances of Alaska and authorized subsistence hunting, fishing, and gathering by rural residents as well as special access provisions on most units. The challenge of ANILCA is to achieve a balance of interests that are often in conflict. Currently, NPCA is working to protect sensitive park areas and wildlife from inappropriate development of roads and unregulated motorized use, and to ensure that our magnificent national parks in

Alaska always offer the sense of wildness, discovery, and adventure that Congress intended.

In 1981, the association sponsored a conference to address serious issues affecting the welfare of the National Park System. The following year, NPCA published a book on this theme called *National Parks in Crisis*. In the 1980s and 1990s, as well, the association sponsored its nationwide "March for Parks" program in conjunction with Earth Day in April. Money raised from the hundreds of marches funds local park projects, including improvement and protection priorities and educational projects in national, state, and local parks.

NPCA's landmark nine-volume document, *National Park System Plan*, was issued in 1988. It contained proposals for new parks and park expansions, assessments of threats to park resources and of research needs, explorations of the importance of interpretation to the visitor's quality of experience, and issues relating to the internal organization of the National Park Service. Two years later, the two-volume *Visitor Impact Management* was released. This document found favor within the National Park Service because of its pragmatic discussions of "carrying capacity" and visitor-impact management methodology and its case studies. In 1993, *Park Waters in Peril* was released, focusing on threats seriously jeopardizing water resources and presenting a dozen case studies.

The association has become increasingly concerned about the effect of noise on the natural quiet in the parks. NPCA has helped formulate restrictions on flightseeing tours over key parts of the Grand Canyon; urged special restrictions on tour flights over Alaska's national parks; supported a ban on tour flights over other national parks such as Yosemite; expressed opposition to plans for construction of major new commercial airports close to Mojave National Preserve and Petroglyph National Monument; opposed the recreational use of snowmobiles in some parks and advocated restrictions on their use in others; and supported regulations prohibiting the use of personal watercraft on lakes in national parks.

Other association activities of the late 20th century have included helping to block development of a major gold mining operation that could have seriously impaired Yellowstone National Park; opposing a coal mine near

Zion National Park that would have polluted Zion Canyon's North Fork of the Virgin River; objecting to proposed lead mining that could pollute the Ozark National Scenic Riverways; opposing a major waste dump adjacent to Joshua Tree National Park; and helping to defeat a proposed U.S. Department of Energy nuclear waste dump adjacent to Canyonlands National Park and on lands worthy of addition to the park. NPCA is currently proposing the completion of this national park with the addition of 500,000 acres. This proposal to double the size of the park would extend protection across the entire Canyonlands Basin. NPCA has also continued to work with the Everglades Coalition and others to help formulate meaningful ways of restoring the seriously impaired Everglades ecosystem; is urging protection of New Mexico's geologically and scenically outstanding Valles Caldera, adjacent to Bandelier National Monument; and is pushing for the installation of scrubbers on air-polluting coal-fired power plants in the Midwest and upwind from the Grand Canyon.

The association, in addition, is continuing to seek meaningful solutions to traffic congestion and urbanization on the South Rim of the Grand Canyon and in Yosemite Valley; is opposing construction of a six-lane highway through Petroglyph National Monument that would destroy sacred Native American cultural assets; and is fighting a plan to build a new road through Denali National Park. NPCA has supported re-establishment of such native wildlife as the gray wolf at Yellowstone and desert bighorn sheep at Capitol Reef and other desert parks, as well as urging increased scientific research that will enable the National Park Service to more effectively protect natural ecological processes in the future. The association is also continuing to explore a proposal to combine Organ Pipe Cactus National Monument and Cabreza Prieta National Wildlife Refuge into a Sonoran Desert National Park, possibly in conjunction with Mexico's Pinacate Biosphere Reserve.

In 1994, on the occasion of NPCA's 75th anniversary, the association sponsored a major conference on the theme "Citizens Protecting America's Parks: Joining Forces for the Future." As a result, NPCA became more active in recruiting a more racially and socially diverse group of park protectors. Rallying new constituencies for the parks helped NPCA in 1995 to defeat a bill that would have called for Congress to review national parks for possible closure. NPCA was also instrumental in the passage of legislation to establish the National Underground Railroad Network to Freedom.

In January 1999, NPCA hosted another major conference, this time focusing on the need for the park system, and the Park Service itself, to be relevant, accessible, and open to all Americans. The conference led to the creation of a number of partnership teams between national parks and minority communities. In conjunction with all this program activity, the association experienced its greatest growth in membership, jumping from about 24,000 in 1980 to nearly 400,000 in the late 1990s.

As NPCA and its committed Board of Trustees, staff, and volunteers face the challenges of park protection in the 21st century, the words of the association's past president, Wallace W. Atwood, in 1929 are as timely now as then:

> All who join our association have the satisfaction that comes only from unselfish acts; they will help carry forward a consistent and progressive program . . . for the preservation and most appropriate utilization of the unique wonderlands of our country. Join and make this work more effective.

Each of us can help nurture one of the noblest endeavors in the entire history of mankind—the national parks idea that began so many years ago at Yellowstone and has spread and blossomed around the world. Everyone can help make a difference in determining just how well we succeed in protecting the priceless and irreplaceable natural and cultural heritage of the National Park System and passing it along unimpaired for the generations to come.

▲ Low tide near Cape Alava in Olympic National Park, Washington

CRATER LAKE NATIONAL PARK

▲ *Whitebark pine*

CRATER LAKE NATIONAL PARK

Crater Lake, OR 97604
541-594-2211, ext. 402

Established in 1902, this 183,224-acre national park atop the crest of the Cascade Mountains in southern Oregon protects Crater Lake, an unusually deep, clear, intensely blue body of water occupying the six-mile-wide caldera of an ancient volcano. Approximately 7,700 years ago, enormous eruptions destroyed most of Mount Mazama, a huge, cone-shaped volcano believed to have risen to around 12,000 feet above sea level—a height similar to that of Mount Rainier in the Washington Cascades. The mountain's base was all that was left after the blast. It now forms the rim of the caldera, a circular basin that subsequently filled with water from springs at the bottom of the crater and from rain and snow-melt. The surface of the lake is at 6,176 feet above sea level, while the rim rises between 500 and 2,000 feet above the lake.

The park's 33-mile Rim Drive (usually closed by snow from mid-October to early July) provides numerous opportunities to view this awesome wonder. With lush conifer forests covering the mountains and valleys surrounding Crater Lake, many of the Rim Drive and trail views of the lake are beautifully framed by mountain hemlocks, Shasta red firs, and white-bark pines.

Because Crater Lake is fed by warm springs at the bottom of the caldera, exploiting the geothermal resources nearby risks impairment of the lake's extraordinary water quality. Consequently, NPCA has strongly opposed plans for geothermal drilling adjacent to this park.

OUTSTANDING FEATURES

Among the many outstanding features of the park are the following: **Crater Lake**, the deepest lake in the United States and the seventh deepest in the world; **Sinnott Memorial Overlook**, an architecturally interesting structure that blends with the landscape on the caldera rim at Rim Village, where park interpreters offer frequent summer talks on the geological history of Crater Lake; **Wizard Island**, a cinder cone rising 764 feet above the western part of the lake; **The Watchman**, a peak with an outstanding viewpoint overlooking Wizard Island; **Hillman Peak**, the central plug of a 70,000-year-old volcano partially exposed by Mount Mazama's collapse and, at 8,151 feet above sea level, the highest point on the rim; **Devil's Backbone**, one of a number of partially exposed outcroppings of resistent rock called dikes—this one extending from rim to lake; **Llao Rock**, the stump of a massive, 1,200-foot-thick lava flow that once poured down Mount Mazama and is exposed in the caldera wall; **Cleetwood Cove**, where a steep, one-mile trail provides the only visitor access to the lake's shore; **Mount Scott**, at 8,929 feet the highest point in the park that affords a grand panorama of Crater Lake and the surrounding area; **Phantom Ship**, a small island that is part of the original volcano's cone, best viewed from the overlook at Kerr Notch; **The Pinnacles**, weird spires and columns of hardened, gas-fused volcanic ash, also called fossil fumaroles, that can be seen from an overlook above Wheeler Creek Canyon, at the end of a seven-mile spur road; and **Vidae Falls**, a beautiful, 100-foot-high cascade.

PRACTICAL INFORMATION

When to Go

Summer, when the color is most vibrant, is the best time to view the lake. Many days are sunny, and rain showers (or even mid-summer snowstorms) are generally short and infrequent. Winter is becoming increasingly popular for recreational activities, but snowfall can be tremendous, reaching depths of 20 feet. While the Rim Drive is normally closed from mid-October to early July, Rim Village is accessible from State Route 62.

How to Get There

By Car: From Klamath Falls, drive north 22 miles on U.S. Route 97, then northwest 29 miles on State Route 62 into the park, then north about four miles to the Rim Drive. From

CRATER LAKE NATIONAL PARK

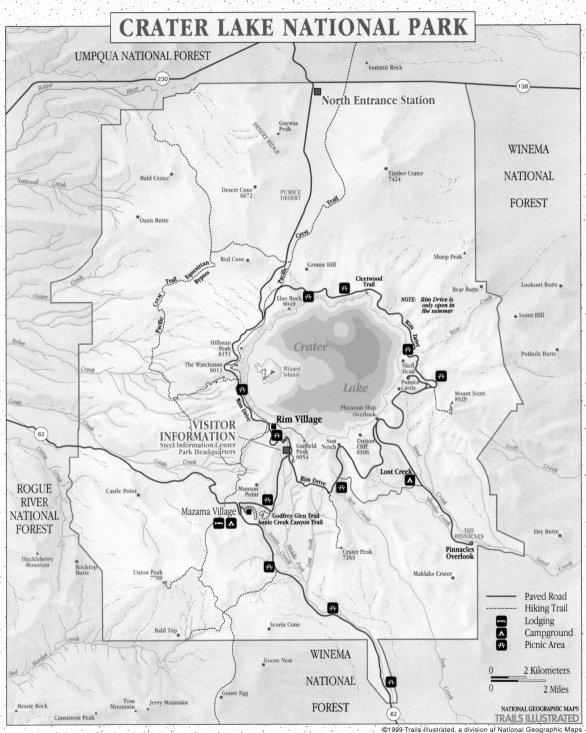

UMPQUA NATIONAL FOREST

230

North Entrance Station

138

Rogue River

Summit Rock

Gaywas Peak

DESERT RIDGE

WINEMA NATIONAL FOREST

Bald Crater

Desert Cone 6672

PUMICE DESERT

Timber Crater 7424

National Creek

Oasis Butte

Trail

Crest

Crest Trail Pacific

Equestrian Bypass

Pacific Crest Trail

Red Cone

Grouse Hill

Sharp Peak

Bear Butte

Lookout Butte

Scout Hill

Crater

Creek

Creek

Bybee

Llao Rock 8049

Cleetwood Trail

NOTE: Rim Drive is only open in the summer

Rim Drive

Bear Creek

Pothole Butte

Hillman Peak 8151

The Watchman 8013

Crater Lake

Wizard Island

Skell Head

Pumice Castle

Mount Scott 8929

Rim Drive

Castle

Creek

Creek

Rim Village

VISITOR INFORMATION
Steel Information Center
Park Headquarters

Garfield Peak 8054

Sun Notch

Phantom Ship Overlook

Dutton Cliff 8106

Scott Creek

62

Castle Creek

Rim Drive

Lost Creek

Wheeler Creek

Dry Butte

ROGUE RIVER NATIONAL FOREST

Castle Point

Munson Point

Mazama Village

Godfrey Glen Trail
Annie Creek Canyon Trail

Sun Creek

Annie Creek

Middle Fork

East Fork

Crater Peak 7263

THE PINNACLES

Pinnacles Overlook

Sand Creek

Huckleberry Mountain

Rocktop Butte

Union Peak 7709

Maklaks Crater

Creek

Bald Top

Scoria Cone

Creek

Blanket

Red

Goose Nest

WINEMA NATIONAL FOREST

Sun Creek

Bessie Rock

Cinnamon Peak

Tom Mountain

Jerry Mountain

Goose Egg

62

Legend

——	Paved Road
- - -	Hiking Trail
🛏	Lodging
⛺	Campground
⛱	Picnic Area

0   2 Kilometers

0   2 Miles

▲ Crater Lake National Park, Oregon

I-5 at Medford, drive northeast 72 miles on State Route 62 and into the park, then north about four miles to the Rim Drive. From I-5 at Roseburg, drive east 85 miles on State Route 138 to the park's north entrance. From U.S. Route 97, drive west 15 miles on State Route 138 to the park's north entrance. Note that the north entrance is open only in summer.

By Air: Flights are available into Portland International Airport (503-335-1234) and Medford-Rogue Valley International Airport (541-772-8068) in Medford, Oregon.

By Train: Amtrak (800-872-7245) stops in Klamath Falls, Oregon.

By Bus: Greyhound Lines (800-231-2222) stops in Medford and Klamath Falls, Oregon.

Fees and Permits

Entrance fees are $10 per vehicle from May through October; passes are valid for seven consecutive days. The fee is $5 for those on foot or bicycle. Free backcountry permits are required; they are available at park visitor centers.

Visitor and Information Centers

Rim Village Visitor Center: open from early June through late September. Interpretive information, publications and backcountry permits.

Steel Information Center: open all year, except Christmas Day. Interpretive exhibits, video, publications, backcountry permits, and post office.

Facilities

Lodging, restaurants, camper's store, service station, showers, and laundry (all open from mid-May to mid-October).

Handicapped Accessibility

Rim Visitor Center, Steel Information Center, restrooms at Rim Village and Mazama Village, Rim Village cafeteria and gift shop, Crater Lake Lodge, and Mazama Village camp store are wheelchair accessible. Snow and ice may impede accessibility at times.

Medical Services

Park rangers provide emergency medical services. Hospitals are located in Klamath Falls, 60 miles from the park, and in Medford, 80 miles away.

Pets

Pets are permitted on leashes not to exceed six feet in length, but are not allowed on trails or in public buildings.

Safety and Regulations

For your safety and enjoyment and for the protection of the park, please follow these regulations and suggestions:

- Because volcanic rock is crumbly and unstable, edges along the caldera rim tend to be extremely hazardous. Visitors are urged to be careful along the rim. Do not cross over or around rock walls and other safety barriers, and keep a close watch on children.

- Persons with heart or respiratory difficulties are cautioned not to overexert themselves at the park's high elevations.

- Motor vehicles are permitted only on designated roads.

- Descents to Crater Lake must be made exclusively on the Cleetwood Trail.

- To avoid attracting bears, campsites should be kept clean, and food should be properly stored.

- Feeding, disturbing, capturing, or hunting wildlife, or damaging plantlife is prohibited.

The National Park Service asks that visitors not litter the park. Remember the excellent slogan to "leave only footprints" as a guide to help protect this national park.

ACTIVITIES

Hiking, birdwatching, interpreter-led hikes, children's programs, summer campfire programs, bicycling, motor launch tours on the lake, fishing, picnicking, camping, cross-country skiing, snowshoeing, and snowmobiling (the latter only on the park's north entrance road). Further information is available in the park's newspaper, *Crater Lake Reflections*.

Hiking Trails

Among the park's 140 miles of hiking trails are
the following: **Annie Creek Trail**, a moderately easy, 1.7-mile, self-guiding interpretive
loop route beginning at Mazama
Campground, looping through Annie Creek
Canyon, following Annie Creek where colorful
summer wildflowers bloom, and passing a few
fumarole pinnacles; **Godfrey Glen Trail**, a
fairly easy 1.5-mile, self-guiding interpretive
route beginning about one mile from the self-

guiding interpretive loop up the road from
State Route 62 to the Rim Drive. Trail winds
through a hemlock-fir forest overlooking
Munson Creek Canyon and numerous pinnacles and spires hardened by the fusion of volcanic ash as hot steam poured from steam
vents, called fumaroles. As at other unstable,
sheer drop-offs in the park, visitors should stay
a safe distance back from edges and keep a
careful watch on children; **Castle Crest
Wildflower Trail**, an easy half-mile loop
route through forest and meadow, beginning

near the Steel Information Center and offering opportunities to see a wide variety of colorful wildflowers in summer; **Garfield Peak Trail**, a strenuous, 1.7-mile, 954-foot climb, beginning at Crater Lake Lodge and providing a magnificent panorama of Crater Lake from this 8,054-foot summit; **The Watchman Peak Trail**, a moderately strenuous, .8-mile, 456-foot climb, beginning at The Watchman Overlook on the Rim Drive, proceeding on an old roadway, and switchbacking up to this 8,013-foot summit, which provides a grand

▲ *Wizard Island, Crater Lake National Park, Oregon*

panorama of Crater Lake; **Cleetwood Trail**, a strenuous, 1.1-mile route that descends steeply from the rim to the tour-boat dock, at the northern edge of Crater Lake (for information on motor launch tours, call 541-594-2511); **Wizard Island Summit Trail**, a fairly strenuous, .9-mile, 764-foot switch-backing climb, from the boat dock to the summit of this island cinder cone; **Mount Scott Trail**, a

◀ *Wizard Island from Hillman Peak in Crater Lake National Park, Oregon*

strenuous, 2.5-mile, 1,200-foot climb, beginning near a picnic area just east of the Cloudcap Overlook spur road junction with the Rim Drive, switch-backing to this 8,929-foot summit (the park's hihest), and affording a vast panorama of Crater Lake from the east and the surrounding area; and **Pacific Crest National Scenic Trail**, a 33-mile segment of this trail, which runs from Canada to Mexico, winds north-south through this park and provides backcountry hiking and horseback riding. An alternate stretch of this trail for hiking only branches and follows some of the western rim of Crater Lake.

OVERNIGHT STAYS

Lodging and Dining

Options include:

Crater Lake Lodge, a large rustic hotel at Rim Village, originally built in 1915, closed and nearly razed in 1989. Fortunately, it was then beautifully rehabilitated to create a feeling of rustic elegance and tasteful charm and was reopened in 1995. Open from about May 20 to October 20. Nicely furnished rooms (many with lake views), delightful dining room (dinner reservations advised), and impressive great hall.

The Watchman Restaurant, buffet at Rim Village during the summer.

Reservations for these places can be made by contacting Crater Lake Company, 1211 Avenue C, White City, OR 97503; 541-830-8700.

The Rim Village cafeteria is open all year.

Mazama Village Motor Inn, near the junction of State Route 62 and the road leading to the Rim Drive, is open from May to October, providing simply furnished rooms.

Lodging Outside the Park

Accommodations are available in such nearby communities as Fort Klamath, Chiloquin, Prospect, Diamond Lake, Klamath Falls, Medford, and Roseburg.

Campgrounds

Sites are available on a first-come, first-served basis, with a 14-day limit. Campers are advised to arrive early in the day to secure a site. The larger Mazama Campground, located near the junction of State Route 62 and the road to the Rim Drive, is open from when the snow melts (usually during mid-June) until it is closed by snow in October. Handicapped-accessible restrooms, water, a camp store, showers, a laundry, and sanitary dump are available. The smaller, more rustic Lost Creek Campground on the Pinnacles road is open from mid-July through September.

Backcountry Camping

Camping is allowed all year throughout much of the park backcountry with a free permit, available at the information and visitor centers. Stock use is limited to the Pacific Crest National Scenic Trail, the Bald Crater Loop, and part of Lightning Spring Trail. Dogs and other pets are not allowed on trails or anywhere else in the backcountry.

FLORA AND FAUNA (Partial Listings)

Mammals: elk (along the southern end of the park), mule and blacktail (subspecies of mule) deer, black bear, mountain lion, bobcat, coyote, red fox, fisher, pine marten, river otter, longtail and shorttail weasels, yellowbelly marmot, badger, porcupine, striped skunk, mountain beaver, snowshoe hare, mountain cottontail, pika, Douglas and golden-mantled squirrels, California ground squirrel, and Townsend and yellow pine chipmunks.

Birds: common merganser, California gull, ruffed and blue grouse, northern goshawk, red-tailed hawk, bald and golden eagles, peregrine falcon, great horned owl, rufous hummingbird, woodpeckers (pileated, downy, and hairy), flicker, horned lark, violet-green swallow, raven, Steller's and gray jays, Clark's nutcracker, mountain chickadee, red-breasted nuthatch, brown creeper, winter and rock wrens, dipper, ruby-crowned and golden-crowned kinglets, robin, Townsend's solitaire, thrushes (Swainson's, hermit, and varied), western and mountain bluebirds, warblers (yellow-rumped, Townsend's, hermit, MacGillivray's, and Wilson's), sparrows (western tanager, white-crowned, golden-crowned, chipping, and Lincoln's), rufous-sided towhee, dark-eyed junco, rosy and Cassin's finches, black-headed and evening grosbeaks, red crossbill, and pine siskin.

Trees, Shrubs, and Flowers: pines (whitebark, sugar, lodgepole, and ponderosa), mountain hemlock, Douglas fir, firs (subalpine, white, and Shasta red), black cottonwood, quaking aspen, bigleaf maple, Pacific mountain ash, Pacific red elder, greenleaf and pinemat manzanitas, currant, snowbush ceanothus, rabbitbrush, false hellebore, Newberry knotweed, glacier and fawn lilies, western pasqueflower, columbine, monkshood, gilia, penstemon, purple lupine, dirty socks (*Eriogonum*), subalpine spirea, forget-me-not, shootingstar, bistort, longleaf arnica, Lewis and dwarf monkeyflowers, paintbrush, groundsel, spreading phlox, and stonecrop.

NEARBY POINTS OF INTEREST

The areas surrounding Crater Lake National Park offer a number of other fascinating attractions that can be enjoyed as day trips or overnight excursions. These include: the Rogue River and Winema national forests, adjoining the park; Oregon Caves National Monument, Redwood National Park, and the U.S. Forest Service's Smith River National Recreation Area, to the southwest; Lava Beds National Monument, Lassen Volcanic National Park, and the U.S. Fish & Wildlife Service's Klamath Marsh, Lower Klamath, and Tule Lake national wildlife refuges, and Whiskeytown-Shasta-Trinity National Recreation Area, to the south; Hart Mountain National Antelope Range and Malheur National Wildlife Refuge, to the east; John Day Fossil Beds National Monument and the Forest Service's Newberry National Volcanic Monument, to the northeast; Mount Hood and the Columbia River Gorge, to the north; and the Forest Service's Oregon Dunes National Recreation Area, to the northwest.

GLACIER NATIONAL PARK

▲ *Sunrise on St. Mary Lake*

Glacier National Park

West Glacier, MT 59936-0128
406-888-7800

This magnificent national park of more than a million acres located in the Rocky Mountains of northwest Montana protects stunningly beautiful mountain peaks along the Continental Divide, along with richly forested valleys, mountain-framed lakes, glaciers, streams, and waterfalls. Elevations in the park range from 3,150 feet above sea level to 10,466 feet atop Mt. Cleveland. A number of major lakes occupy long narrow basins that were carved and shaped by ancient glaciers. The breathtakingly scenic, 50-mile Going-to-the-Sun Road passes the two largest lakes and crosses over 6,646-foot Logan Pass in the park's central area. Other roads lead to several other major lakes, while just over 730 miles of hiking and horseback riding trails offer opportunities to explore the park's wilderness areas.

Established in 1910, Glacier became part of the Waterton-Glacier International Peace Park, with Canada's adjoining 130,000-acre Waterton Lakes National Park, in 1932. It was designated a Biosphere Reserve in 1976. The park's tremendous ecological diversity supports more than 60 species of mammals, 200 kinds of birds, and 1,000 varieties of trees, flowers, and other plantlife.

OUTSTANDING FEATURES

Among the many outstanding features of the park are the following: **Lake McDonald**, an 11-mile-long, 472-foot-deep lake—the park's largest—on the lush west side of the Continental Divide; **McDonald Falls**, a thundering waterfall on McDonald Creek that can be seen from the Going-to-the-Sun Road; **The Garden Wall**, an enormous, narrow ridge along the Continental Divide, below which the Going-to-the-Sun Road switchbacks above timberline, amid a scene of towering peaks; **Logan Pass**, the highest point on the Going-to-the-Sun Road, where mountain goats are often seen and the starting point for a short

hike to a viewpoint overlooking Hidden Lake; **St. Mary Lake**, a ten-mile-long, 300-foot-deep lake framed by spectacular glacier-carved peaks on the park's drier east side; **Swiftcurrent** and **Josephine lakes**, two sparkling gems below awesome Mount Gould and other encircling peaks in the northeast part of the park; **Blackfoot**, **Grinnell**, and **Sperry glaciers**, the park's three largest; **Two Medicine Lake**, with imposing Sinopah Mountain rising from its shore, in the park's southeast corner; **Bowman**, **Kintla**, and **Upper Kintla lakes**, in the richly forested northwest corner of the park; and **Upper Waterton Lake**, extending for miles in both Glacier and Waterton Lakes national parks.

PRACTICAL INFORMATION

When to Go

The park is open year-round. Summer through early autumn is the best time to visit, although visitors who wish to experience solitude may prefer winter, when less than 5 percent of the park's visitors come. September is usually especially delightful, with few crowds and touches of autumn foliage colors. Trails are usually clear of snow by mid-June at lower elevations and by mid-July at higher elevations. Going-to-the-Sun Road and Chief Mountain International Highway are both open in summer; portions are closed in winter.

How to Get There

By Car: To Going-to-the-Sun Road: from U.S. Route 93 at Kalispell, drive northeast 33 miles on U.S. Route 2 to West Glacier, and north 2 miles into the park; from U.S. Route 2 at Browning, drive northwest 31 miles to St. Mary, and west into the park. To Two Medicine Lake area: from U.S. Route 2 at East Glacier Park, drive north 4 miles on State Route 49, and west about 6 miles to the park. To Many Glacier area: from U.S. Route 89 at Babb, drive west about 5 miles.

By Air: Flights are available into Glacier Park International Airport (406-257-5994) in Kalispell and Johnson Bell Missoula Airport (406-728-4381) in Missoula.

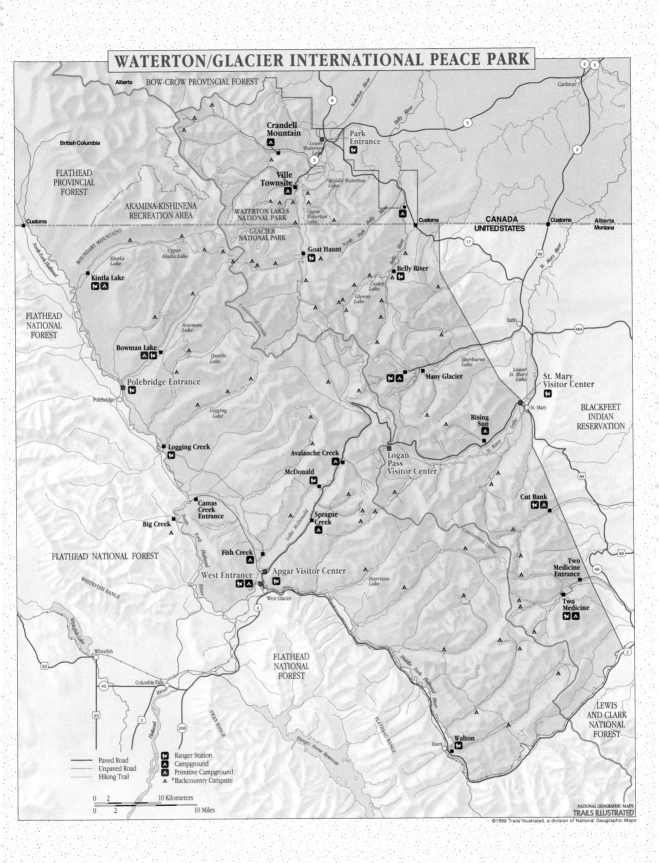

WATERTON/GLACIER INTERNATIONAL PEACE PARK

Alberta
BOW-CROW PROVINCIAL FOREST

Cardston

British Columbia

Crandell Mountain

Lower Waterton Lake

Park Entrance

FLATHEAD PROVINCIAL FOREST

Ville Townsite

AKAMINA-KISHINENA RECREATION AREA

Middle Waterton Lake

WATERTON LAKES NATIONAL PARK

Upper Waterton Lake

Customs

Customs

CANADA
UNITED STATES

Customs

Alberta
Montana

GLACIER NATIONAL PARK

North Fork Belly River

Belly River

St. Mary River

FLATHEAD NATIONAL FOREST

BOUNDARY MOUNTAINS

Kintla Lake

Upper Kintla Lake

Goat Haunt

Cosley Lake

Belly River

Glenns Lake

Babb

Kintla Lake

Continental Divide

Bowman Lake

FLATHEAD NATIONAL FOREST

Quartz Lake

Sherburne Lake

Lower St. Mary Lake

St. Mary Visitor Center

BLACKFEET INDIAN RESERVATION

Bowman Lake

Many Glacier

Polebridge Entrance

Polebridge

Logging Lake

St. Mary

Logging Creek

Rising Sun

St. Mary Lake

Avalanche Creek

Logan Pass Visitor Center

McDonald

Cut Bank

Camas Creek Entrance

Lake McDonald

Sprague Creek

Continental Divide

Big Creek

Two Medicine Entrance

Fish Creek

Harrison Lake

Two Medicine

West Entrance

Apgar Visitor Center

West Glacier

WHITEFISH RANGE

North Fork Flathead River

Whitefish Lake

Whitefish

Columbia Falls

Flathead River

FLATHEAD NATIONAL FOREST

FLATHEAD RANGE

Middle Fork Flathead River

LEWIS AND CLARK NATIONAL FOREST

SWAN RANGE

Hungry Horse Reservoir

Essex

Walton

Legend:
— Paved Road
— Unpaved Road
···· Hiking Trail

🏠 Ranger Station
🏕 Campground
▲ Primitive Campground
▲ *Backcountry Campsite

0   2   10 Kilometers
0   2   10 Miles

NATIONAL GEOGRAPHIC MAPS
TRAILS ILLUSTRATED
©1999 Trails Illustrated, a division of National Geographic Maps

▲ *St. Mary Lake in Glacier National Park, Montana*

By Train: Amtrak (800-872-7245) stops at the Glacier Park Station and at East Glacier (limited service), Essex, West Glacier, and Whitefish.

By Bus: Greyhound Lines (800-231-2222) and the Intermountain Bus Company (406-755-4011) serve Great Falls, Missoula, and Kalispell.

Fees and Permits

Entrance fees, valid for seven consecutive days, are $10 per vehicle and $5 per person on foot, bicycle, motorcycle, or by bus. Permits required for backcountry camping are available at visitor centers and ranger stations.

Visitor Centers and Museums

St. Mary Visitor Center: open daily from Memorial Day through September. Interpretive exhibits, publications, and maps.

Logan Pass Visitor Center: open daily from mid-June to mid-September (as weather permits). Interpretive exhibits, publications, and maps.

Apgar Visitor Center: open daily from late May through October and winter weekends. Interpretive exhibits, publications, and maps.

Facilities

Camp stores are located at Apgar, Lake McDonald, Swiftcurrent, Rising Sun, and Two Medicine. Food and supplies are available at West Glacier and East Glacier Park and St. Mary. Service stations are located near Apgar and St. Mary campgrounds.

Handicapped Accessibility

Most visitor centers and exhibits, Trail of the Cedars, Apgar Nature Trail, and restrooms at Apgar, Avalanche, Fish Creek, Many Glacier, Rising Sun, Sprague Creek, and St. Mary campgrounds and all group campgrounds are wheelchair accessible. Printed texts, guided walks, slide shows, and TDD service (406-888-5790) are available for the hearing impaired, and a taped park brochure is available for the visually impaired. Contact park headquarters or a visitor center for a complete accessibility guide.

Medical Services

First aid is available in the park. A hospital is located in Whitefish, 25 miles west of the park.

Pets

Pets must be leashed at all times and are not allowed on trails, in the backcountry, or in public buildings. Owners of guide dogs should check in at a ranger station before using backcountry trails.

Climate

Glacier's climate is characterized by cool temperatures and extended winters (snow has fallen in every month of the year). Higher elevations will have greater precipitation and lower temperatures. In some areas, seasonal snowfall may exceed 1,000 inches. Average daily temperature range in Fahrenheit and average daily precipitation for lower elevation areas are as follows:

Month	AVERAGE DAILY	
	Temperature (F)	Precipitation
January	11-27°	2.7 inches
February	15-33°	1.9 inches
March	20-39°	1.6 inches
April	28-52°	1.6 inches
May	36-63°	1.7 inches
June	44-69°	2.2 inches
July	47-79°	1.2 inches
August	46-77°	1.3 inches
September	39-66°	1.3 inches
October	32-55°	1.9 inches
November	2-39°	2.3 inches
December	7-32°	2.8 inches

Safety and Regulations

For your safety and enjoyment and for the protection of the park, please follow these regulations and suggestions:

- Vehicles must remain on established roads. Vehicle size limitations of 20 feet long by 7.5 feet wide are in effect on a portion of Going-to-the-Sun Road. For those who prefer not to drive, shuttle buses and red-and-black "jammer" bus tours are available.

- Because storms can develop quickly, hikers are urged to be prepared with rain gear, warm clothing, and high-energy foods. The National Park Service advises hikers to leave their intended itinerary with a ranger and never enter the backcountry alone.

- During thunderstorms, avoid snowfields and open, high ridges and peaks, and isolated tall trees. Avalanches are also possible in winter and spring.

- Lake and stream water is extremely cold and rocks may be slippery, so visitors are urged to use caution and to keep children away from swift currents.

- Persons with heart or respiratory difficulties should be careful to avoid overexertion, especially at the park's higher elevations.

- Feeding, disturbing, capturing, or hunting wildlife and damaging trees or other plantlife is prohibited. Visitors are strongly urged to familiarize themselves with safety information (available at all park entrances and visitor centers) concerning bears and other wild animals. Grizzly bears can be especially dangerous.

The National Park Service asks that visitors not litter the park. Remember the excellent slogan to "leave only footprints" as a guide to help protect this national park.

ACTIVITIES

In addition to activities described below, park visitors can participate in mountain climbing, river rafting (offered by private companies), birdwatching, ski touring, bus tours, picnicking, and camping. Free interpreter-led activities include walks and hikes, talks and slide shows, and campfire programs. Educational field seminars are offered by the nonprofit Glacier Institute; for information, write the institute at P.O. Box 1457B, Kalispell, MT 59903.

Boating

Boating is permitted on some lakes; motor size is restricted to 10 hp on most lakes. Excursion boat cruises are offered at Many Glacier, Rising Sun, Upper Waterton Lake, Two Medicine, and Lake McDonald. Canoeing is popular on some lakes; rentals are available.

Horseback Riding

Scheduled, guided trips are available at Many Glacier, Lake McDonald Lodge, and Apgar. Visitors with their own horses should request the free brochure on regulations regarding private stock use in the park.

Bicycling

Bicycling is restricted in the most hazardous parts of the Going-to-the-Sun Road during peak traffic periods (from June 15 to Labor Day) because of narrow and winding stretches with little or no shoulders. Bicyclists should stay on established roads or designated routes. It is best to bicycle Going-to-the-Sun Road from east to west.

Fishing

Fishing licenses are not required within the park, although licenses are required for Blackfeet Reservation, which is adjacent to the park boundary. A free folder on fishing regulations is available on request; it is the visitor's responsibility to comply with all regulations. Water is extremely cold and swift in many areas, and it is important to be cautious, especially around slippery rocks.

Hiking

The approximately 730 miles of trails in the park are usually passable at the lower elevations by mid-June and at higher elevations by mid-July. The National Park Service urges hikers to stay on marked trails and avoid crossing steep snow banks. Overnight excursions require a backcountry permit, available on a first-come, first-served basis, obtained at least 24 hours in advance.

And remember: this is BEAR COUNTRY! Hikers are urged to become informed about bears and learn ways to stay alert and reduce the chances of harm. The National Park

Service, which includes information in its *Waterton-Glacier Guide* newspaper, urges: "Don't Surprise Bears! Bears will usually move out of the way if they hear people approaching, so make noise. Most bells are not loud enough. Calling out or clapping hands loudly at regular intervals are better ways to make your presence known."

Shorter Hiking Trails

Among shorter trails available are: **Trail of the Cedars**, an easy half-mile, self-guided interpretive, wheelchair accessible, boardwalk loop beginning just north of the Avalanche Campground entrance on the Going-to-the-Sun Road and passing through a beautiful old-growth forest of western red cedars and western hemlocks. Trail provides a view of scenic Avalanche Creek Gorge; **Hidden Lake Nature Trail**, a fairly easy, 1.5-mile, self-guided interpretive boardwalk route beginning from behind the Logan Pass Visitor Center, leading across the Continental Divide, and providing a breathtaking view from Hidden Lake Overlook of peaks rising high above the exquisite lake nestled in a glacial cirque. Trail also offers the possibility of seeing mountain goats and, in season, a magnificent display of tundra wildflowers (visitors are urged to stay on the trail and avoid trampling the fragile alpine plantlife). Persons with heart or respiratory difficulties should be aware that this trail, while easy, is at approximately 6,650 feet above sea level; **Sun Point/Baring Falls Trail**, an easy .8-mile route beginning at the Sun Point parking area, leading through a Douglas-fir forest on the north shore of St. Mary Lake, and ending at Baring Falls. A trail branches off to spectacularly scenic Going-to-the-Sun Point; **Running Eagle Trail**, an easy .3-mile route beginning just north of the Two Medicine Road bridge over Two Medicine Creek, winding through an Engelmann-spruce and Douglas-fir forest, and ending at intriguing Trick Falls; **Swiftcurrent Lake Trail**, a fairly easy, 2.6-mile loop beginning at the picnic area between Swiftcurrent Lake and Many Glacier Campground, circling counterclockwise around Swiftcurrent Lake with magnificent views of Grinnell Point, Mount Gould, and other grand peaks, and ending just south of Many Glacier Hotel. An alternate route begins

near the hotel and goes clockwise around the lake; **Swiftcurrent Lake-to-Josephine Lake Trail**, an easy quarter-mile, paved path through the forest, connecting with spectacularly scenic boat cruises on these beautiful lakes (there is a fee for boat rides). A trail also encircles Josephine Lake, connecting with the trail leading to Grinnell Lake; **Josephine Lake-to-Grinnell Lake Trail**, an easy one-mile route from the boat dock at the upper end of Josephine Lake to Grinnell Lake; **Ptarmigan Falls Trail**, a fairly easy, 2.5-mile route beginning near the cabins just east of the Swiftcurrent camp store and ending at this beautiful waterfall; and **Rainbow Falls Trail**, an easy, nearly one-mile route beginning near Goat Haunt boat dock, at the south (U.S.) end of Upper Waterton Lake (which is reached by tour boat from the village of Waterton Park, Canada). After winding through lodgepole pine forest along the Waterton River, the trail ends at beautiful Rainbow Falls.

Longer Hiking Trails

Among longer trails available are: **Apgar Lookout Trail**, a fairly strenuous, 2.8-mile route beginning one-third mile north of the park's west entrance on an old road closed to motor vehicles and switchbacking on the trail to the summit of Apgar Mountain; **Avalanche Lake Trail**, a fairly strenuous, 2.8-mile route beginning at Avalanche Creek Campground on the Trail of the Cedars, branching onto Avalanche Lake Trail, climbing through lush forest with views of Avalanche Creek and its waterfalls, and ending at Avalanche Lake, which occupies a glacier-carved basin of a cirque; **Gunsight Pass Trail**, a strenuous, 18.7-mile overnight route beginning at Jackson Glacier overlook, on the Going-to-the-Sun Road; passing Deadwood Falls and upper St. Mary River; crossing over the Continental Divide at 6,946-foot Gunsight Pass; passing Lake Ellen Wilson; reaching the Sperry Chalets (for which advance reservations are required); and descending to Lake McDonald, on the Going-to-the-Sun Road; **Highline Trail**, a strenuous, 11.6-mile route beginning across the Going-to-the-Sun Road from the Logan Pass Visitor Center parking area, partly paralleling the Continental Divide

▲ Avalanche Lake in Glacier National Park, Montana

while passing through some of the park's most magnificent high country, and ending at "The Loop," on the Going-to-the-Sun Road. The trail offers possible opportunities to see mountain goats, bighorn sheep, and alpine wildflowers; **Dawson-Pitamakan Passes Trail**, a strenuous, 16.9-mile two- to three-day loop beginning and ending at Two Medicine Campground, proceeding along the north shore of Two Medicine Lake, crossing over Dawson and Pitamaken passes, going by Oldman Lake, and descending along Dry Fork Creek; **Grinnell Glacier Trail**, a strenuous, 5.5-mile route beginning at the picnic area on Many Glacier Road between Many Glacier Hotel and Many Glacier Campground, proceeding along the shores of Swiftcurrent and Josephine lakes, and climbing to the base of massive Grinnell Glacier. The National Park Service offers interpreter-guided hikes to this glacier, the park's largest; **Iceberg Lake Trail**, a moderately strenuous, 5-mile route beginning near the cabins just east of the Swiftcurrent camp store, proceeding on the trail to Ptarmigan Falls, and continuing to this gem of a lake; and **Boulder Pass Trail**, a strenuous, 36.6-mile, three- to four-day excursion through ruggedly magnificent park wilderness beginning at the foot of Kintla Lake, following the north shores of Kintla and Upper Kintla lakes, crossing over Boulder Pass, and ending at the foot of Bowman Lake. Alternatively, the trail may be hiked in the opposite direction. Hikers should be especially alert for grizzly bears on this trail.

OVERNIGHT STAYS

Lodging and Dining

The following hotels, lodges, and cabins are open from June to mid-September; exact dates may vary. Information and reservations can be made through Glacier Park, Inc., East Glacier, MT 59434, 602-207-6000 (mid-May to mid-October), and Glacier Park, Inc., VIAD Corporate Center, Phoenix, AZ 85077, 602-207-6000 (mid-October to mid-May).

Glacier Park Lodge, a large, rustic, Swiss chalet-style hotel dating from 1913, at East Glacier Park (just outside the national park), offering rooms, elegant dining room, majestic great hall featuring massive Douglas-fir log columns, cocktail lounge, small general store, gift shop, heated swimming pool, golf course, bus tours, and meeting rooms.

Lake McDonald Lodge, a rustic, Swiss chalet-style lodge dating from 1914 and beautifully renovated in 1988-89, along the south shore of Lake McDonald on the Going-to-the-Sun Road, offering rooms and cabins, dining room, impressive lobby featuring tall cedar logs, cocktail lounge, gift shop, general store, and boat rentals.

Rising Sun Motor Inn, above the north shore of St. Mary Lake on the Going-to-the-Sun Road, offering rooms, cabins, and restaurant.

Many Glacier Hotel, a large, rustic, Swiss chalet-style hotel dating from 1915, on the shore of Swiftcurrent Lake, offering rooms and suites (some with lake-view balconies), dining room, impressive great hall featuring tall cedar logs, cocktail lounge, gift shop, small general store, canoe rentals, and boat tours.

Swiftcurrent Motor Inn, at the end of Many Glacier Road, offering simply furnished rooms and cabins (some without bathroom), restaurant, and laundry.

Village Inn, a motel-type structure, in Apgar, at the west end of Lake McDonald, offering rooms, some with kitchenettes.

For room or cabin reservations at *Apgar Village Lodge,* near the park's west entrance, contact the lodge at P.O. Box 398, West Glacier, MT 59936, 406-888-5484.

Lodging Outside the Park

Lodging located outside park boundaries can be found in communities such as East Glacier Park (see Glacier Park Lodge left), Browning, Essex, West Glacier, Corum, Hungry Horse, Columbia Falls, WhiteFish, and Kalispell. Especially during the peak season, please consider using these facilities to decrease visitor impact on the park. Waterton Lakes National Park in Alberta, Canada, also has accommodations at the chalet-style Prince of Wales Hotel dating from 1927, with a grand view of

Upper Waterton Lake, and offering rooms, dining room, Tudor-style great hall, and gift shop. Room reservations for the hotel are made through Glacier Park, Inc. (see left, under Lodging and Dining).

Campgrounds

Campsites at Fish Creek Campground, near Lake McDonald on the park's west side, and St. Mary Campground, near St. Mary Lake on the east side, are available by reservation; call the National Park Reservation Service at 800-365-CAMP. Sites at the other campgrounds are available on a first-come, first-served basis. Because campgrounds are often full in July, August, and early September, campers should arrive early in the day to secure a site. Limit of stay for July and August is seven days. During the rest of the year, the limit is 14 days. Water and flush toilets, where provided, are available from the opening of the campground until mid-September. The rest of the season, water is not available, and pit toilets are provided.

Because Glacier National Park is bear country, campers are urged to keep a clean camp. Visitors should also avoid approaching wildlife: all wild animals should be viewed and photographed from a discreet distance. If you cause an animal to change its behavior, you are too close! This park contains grizzly bears and mountain lions, so it is extremely important to keep small children close to you while camping and hiking. Build fires only in fireplaces provided, and make sure they are out and cold before leaving the campground. A pamphlet containing camping regulations may be obtained at visitor centers, park headquarters, entrance stations, and ranger stations.

Backcountry Camping

During the summer camping season, May 1 to November 20, backcountry permits may be obtained up to 24 hours in advance on a first-come, first-served basis from visitor centers, ranger stations, and park headquarters. Competition is keen for backcountry sites in July and August, so campers should be prepared to accept alternative trip plans. For safety, it is important to cook in designated cooking sites, camp in designated camping sites, and hang food from hanging devices.

FLORA AND FAUNA (Partial Listings)

Mammals: mountain goat, Rocky Mountain bighorn sheep, elk, moose, mule and whitetail deer, grizzly and black bears, mountain lion, lynx, gray wolf, coyote, red fox, wolverine, pine marten, mink, hoary marmot, badger, shorttail and longtail weasels, porcupine, striped skunk, beaver, muskrat, snowshoe hare, pika, red and golden-mantled squirrels, Columbian ground squirrel, and chipmunks (least, redtail, and yellow pine).

Birds: common loon, grebes (horned, eared, and western), tundra swan, Canada goose, mallard, wigeon, ring-necked duck, common and Barrow's goldeneyes, bufflehead, common merganser, coot, California and ring-billed gulls, great blue heron, killdeer, common snipe, spotted sandpiper, grouse (ruffed, blue, and spruce), white-tailed ptarmigan, sharp-shinned and red-tailed hawks, bald and golden eagles, osprey, kestrel, barred and great horned owls, northern pygmy-owl, belted kingfisher, nighthawk, rufous and Calliope hummingbirds, woodpeckers (pileated, downy, hairy, and three-toed), flicker, red-naped sapsucker, eastern and western kingbirds, flycatchers (olive-sided, willow, dusky, and Hammond's), western wood pewee, American pipit, Vaux's swift, swallows (tree, northern rough-winged, bank, violet-green, barn, and cliff), crow, raven, Steller's and gray jays, Clark's nutcracker, chickadees (mountain, black-capped, chestnut-backed, and boreal), red-breasted nuthatch, brown creeper, winter wren, dipper, ruby-crowned and golden-crowned kinglets, robin, thrushes (varied, Swainson's, and hermit), mountain bluebird, cedar and Bohemian waxwings, solitary and warbling vireos, warblers (yellow-rumped, Townsend's, MacGillivray's, yellow, yellowthroat, and Wilson's), northern waterthrush, red-winged blackbird, western meadowlark, western tanager, sparrows (white-crowned, chipping, fox, vesper, and savannah), dark-eyed junco, gray-crowned rosy finch, lazuli bunting, red crossbill, redpoll, Cassin's finch, pine and evening grosbeaks, and pine siskin.

Amphibians and Reptiles: tiger salamander, leopard frog, western painted turtle, and garter snake.

Trees, Shrubs, and Flowers: pines (western white, whitebark, limber, lodgepole, and ponderosa), western larch, white and Engelmann spruces, western hemlock, Douglas fir, subalpine and grand firs, western red cedar, Rocky Mountain juniper, Pacific yew, water and paper birches, Sitka and mountain alders, balsam poplar, black cottonwood, quaking aspen, willow, Rocky Mountain maple, chokecherry, pin cherry, mountainspray, hawthorne, globe and dwarf huckleberries, bog cranberry, thimbleberry, elderberry, gooseberry, serviceberry, devil's club, sagebrush, shrubby cinquefoil, beargrass (a lily), glacier lily, fireweed, kinnikinnick (bearberry), bunchberry, prince's pine, moss campion, cushion phlox, mountain Douglasia (primrose), stonecrop, arnica, sky pilot, groundsel, shootingstar, explorer's gentian, fairyslipper (calypso) orchid, mountain lady's-slipper, monkeyflowers (pink, red, and yellow), Jones columbine, lupine, iris, silky phacelia, blue camas, pasqueflower, queenscup, Indian paintbrush, yellow owlclover, gillardia, wood nymph, yellow and purple violets, and smooth aster.

NEARBY POINTS OF INTEREST

In the area surrounding Glacier National Park, many fascinating attractions can be enjoyed as day trips or overnight excursions. Canada's Waterton Lakes National Park, part of the Waterton-Glacier International Peace Park, is adjacent to the north. For additional information about that park, contact the superintendent at Waterton Park, Alberta TOK 2MO, Canada, 403-859-2224. Akamina-Kishinena Provincial Park, British Columbia, also adjoins the park to the north. Flathead and the Lewis and Clark national forests adjoin the park to the west and south; the Blackfeet Indian Reservation with the Museum of the Plains Indian near Browning adjoins the park to the east; The Nature Conservancy's Pine Butte Swamp Preserve, near Choteau, is about 60 miles to the southeast; and Benton Lake National Wildlife Refuge, near Great Falls, is about 100 miles to the southeast.

MOUNT RAINIER NATIONAL PARK

▲ *Mount Rainier framed by evergreens*

Mount Rainier National Park

**Tahoma Woods, Star Route
Ashford, WA 98304-9751
360-569-2211**

This 235,612-acre national park in the Cascade Mountains of west-central Washington state protects the towering volcanic cone of Mount Rainier. This spectacular, 14,411-foot-high, dormant volcano had its last major eruption 2,000 years ago and is believed to have experienced at least a dozen minor eruptions during the 19th century. Volcanic heat coming from steam vents in the summit's crater demonstrates that the great volcano is not extinct now. According to geologists, the enormous peak could erupt again at any time, as did Mount St. Helens in 1980, less than 50 miles to the south.

This magnificent park was established in 1899 as the nation's fifth national park. In it, Mount Rainier is ringed with 26 glaciers radiating from the summit—the largest single-peak glacier system in the lower 48 states. Below the reach of glacial ice and snowfields are fir-framed, subalpine meadows that blossom with colorful summer wildflowers, dense mountain conifer forests, sparkling lakes, numerous streams and waterfalls, and lush lowland temperate rainforest. More than 50 species of mammals, at least 125 kinds of birds, and nearly 800 varieties of plantlife have been recorded in the park's ecologically diverse habitats.

the Nisqually Vista Trail, from which tall conifers frame an intimate view of Mount Rainier; **Nisqually Glacier**, the most accessible and most monitored of Mount Rainier's many glaciers, the lower end of which is near Paradise; **Narada Falls**, the spot where the Paradise River plunges 168 feet from the edge of an ancient lava flow; the **Tatoosh Range**, a series of jagged peaks in the southern part of the park; **Box Canyon**, a 150-foot-deep slot of a gorge carved by the Muddy Fork of the Cowlitz River at a bend in the Stevens Canyon Road; **Grove of the Patriarchs**, a magnificent, old-growth stand of cedars, hemlocks, and Douglas firs along the Ohanapecosh River in the park's southeast corner, which rivals the virgin-growth coast redwoods in northern California; **Tipsoo Lake**, a meadow- and fir-framed jewel near the Chinook Pass entrance that reflects Mount Rainier's spectacular east side; **Sunrise**, at 6,400 feet above sea level, the park's highest point accessible by road, which winds through Yakima Park's subalpine meadows dotted with clumps of firs and provides breathtaking views of the mountain's magnificent east side; **Emmons Glacier**, the largest glacier in the contiguous United States, covering more than four square miles, on the northeast side of the peak; **Nisqually River**, which descends through a lush, old-growth, lowland conifer forest in the southwest corner of the park; **Reflection Lake**, which is bordered by forest, capturing on its mirror surface a reflection of mountain's south side; and the **Carbon River**, in the northwest corner of the park, flowing through a luxuriant temperate rainforest of giant Douglas firs, western hemlocks, and Sitka spruces.

OUTSTANDING FEATURES

Among the many outstanding features of the park are the following: **Mount Rainier**, the fifth highest mountain in the lower 48 states, the highest peak in the Cascade Mountains, and the awesome centerpiece of this national park; **Paradise**, an exquisitely beautiful landscape of fir-dotted subalpine meadows providing close-up views of the south side of Mount Rainier; **Fairy Pool**, a small body of water on

PRACTICAL INFORMATION

When to Go

The park is open year-round. However, in winter, all roads are closed except the 18 miles between the southwest entrance and Paradise. Summer is usually very pleasant, with average daytime highs in the 70s and cool evenings. Winter temperatures are around the mid-20s, and snowstorms are frequent at higher elevations. The best time for viewing wildflowers is

MOUNT RAINIER NATIONAL PARK

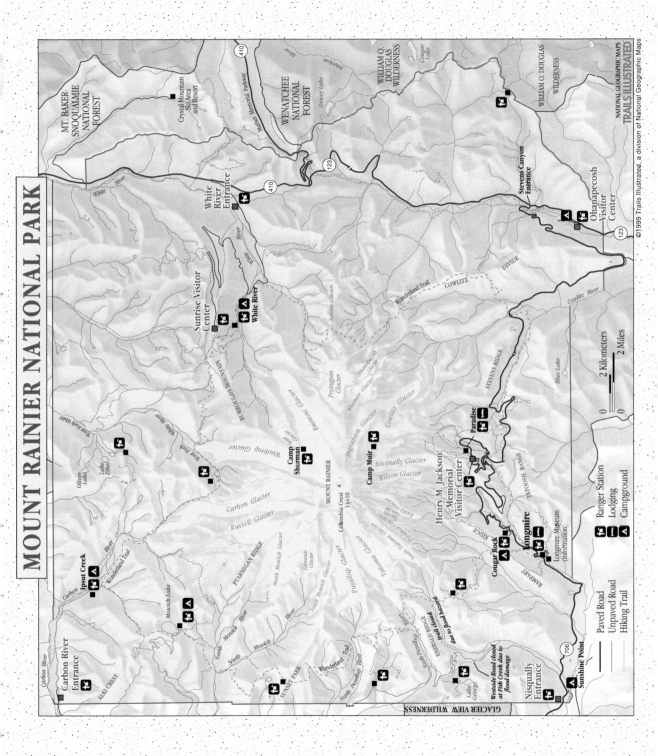

MT. BAKER-
SNOQUALMIE
NATIONAL
FOREST

Crystal Mountain
Ski Area
and Resort

WENATCHEE
NATIONAL
FOREST

WILLIAM O.
DOUGLAS
WILDERNESS

Cougar
Lake

WILLIAM O. DOUGLAS
WILDERNESS

Dewey Lake

Mather Memorial Parkway

White River

410

123

Stevens Canyon
Entrance

Ohanapecosh
Visitor
Center

123

White River
Entrance

410

Sunrise Visitor
Center

White River

White River

BURROUGHS MOUNTAIN

Sarvus Glaciers

Wonderland Trail

COWLITZ

DIVIDE

Cowlitz River

Fryingpan
Glacier

Ohanapecosh
Glacier

Whitman Glacier

Ingraham Glacier

Cowlitz Glacier

STEVENS RIDGE

Blue Lake

West Fork White River

Lake
Elbel

Oliver Lake

Winthrop Glacier

Emmons Glacier

Camp
Shurman

Nisqually Glacier

Wilson Glacier

Camp Muir

Paradise

Henry M. Jackson
Memorial
Visitor Center

0   2 Kilometers
0   2 Miles

MOUNT RAINIER
Columbia Crest
14410

Carbon Glacier

Russell Glacier

PTARMIGAN RIDGE

North Mowich Glacier

Edmunds Glacier

South Mowich Glacier

Puyallup Glacier

Tahoma Glacier

South Tahoma Glacier

Pyramid Glacier

Kautz Glacier

PATOOSH RANGE

Longmire

RIDGE

Longmire Museum
(information)

RAMPART

Cougar Rock

Carbon River

Carbon River
Entrance

Ipsut Creek

Wonderland Trail

Mowich Lake

North Mowich River

South Mowich River

Mowich River

North Puyallup River

South Puyallup River

ENBALD RIDGE

Wonderland Trail

SUNSET PARK

Lake
George

trail closed
due to flood hazard

Westside Road closed
at Fish Creek due to
flood damage

Nisqually
Entrance

706

Sunshine Point

ALKU CREST

GLACIER VIEW WILDERNESS

NATIONAL GEOGRAPHIC MAPS
TRAILS ILLUSTRATED

©1999 Trails Illustrated, a division of National Geographic Maps

Ranger Station

Lodging

Campground

Paved Road

Unpaved Road

Hiking Trail

46

▲ *Mount Rainier National Park, Washington*

in July and August. In all seasons, visitors should be prepared for a variety of weather conditions. Mount Rainier is, in itself, a weather maker, so plan for sudden changes, dress in layers, and always carry rain gear.

How to Get There

By Car: For the Longmire (southwest) entrance: from I-5 exit 127 at Tacoma, drive east 2 miles on State Route 512, south 35 miles on State Route 7 to Elbe, and east 13 miles on State Route 706. From I-5 exit 68, drive east 31 miles on U.S. Route 12 to Morton, north 17 miles on State Route 7 to Elbe, and east 13 miles on State Route 706. To the Ohanapecosh (southeast) entrance: from I-5 exit 68, drive east 72 miles on U.S. Route 12, and north 3 miles on State Route 123. From I-82 exit 31 at Yakima, drive west 64 miles on U.S. Route 12 and north 3 miles on State Route 123. For the Chinook Pass (east) entrance: from I-82 exit 31 at Yakima, drive northwest 17 miles on U.S. Route 12 and west 48 miles on State Route 410. For the White River (northeast) entrance: from I-5 exit 142 (just north of Tacoma), drive east 5 miles on State Route 18 to Auburn, southeast 15 miles on State Route 164, and southeast 34 miles on State Route 410.

By Air: Seattle-Tacoma International Airport (206-431-4444) and Portland International Airport (503-335-1234) are served by major airlines.

By Train: Amtrak (800-872-7245) stops in Seattle, Tacoma, Olympia, Centralia, Longview, Vancouver, Portland, Yakima, and Ellensburg.

By Bus: Greyhound Lines (800-231-2222) stops in major towns and cities. Gray Line Tours (800-426-7532) runs buses to the park from mid-spring to mid-fall from Tacoma and Seattle.

Fees and Permits

Entrance fees, valid for seven consecutive days, are $10 per vehicle and $5 per person on foot, bicycle, motorcycle, or by bus. Free backcountry camping permits available at visitor centers and ranger stations are required. For even short climbs, hikers must register with a park ranger before ascending Mount Rainier.

Visitor Centers and Museum

Longmire Museum: open daily year-round. Interpretive exhibits, publications, and maps.

Wilderness Information Center, at Longmire: open daily from mid-June through September. Information on weather and trail conditions. Wilderness permits for backcountry excursions.

Henry M. Jackson Memorial Visitor Center, at Paradise: open daily from May to mid-October and on weekends and holidays the rest of the year. Interpretive exhibits, audio-visual programs, publications, maps, hot showers, and a grill.

Ohanapecosh Visitor Center: open daily from Memorial Day through mid-October and on weekends the rest of the year. Interpretive exhibits, slide shows, publications, and maps.

Sunrise Visitor Center: open daily from July to mid-September. Interpretive exhibits, programs, publications, and maps.

White River Wilderness Information Center: open in summer. Trail information and backcountry permits.

Facilities

Lodging, restaurants, limited groceries and camping supplies, gift shops, post offices (at Paradise and National Park inns), picnic areas, campgrounds, and hot showers. There are no service stations within the park.

Handicapped Accessibility

All visitor centers and the Longmire Museum, Cougar Rock Campground, picnic areas, and portions of trails near Jackson Visitor Center are wheelchair accessible. Both Paradise and National Park inns have accessible rooms. For detailed information, contact park headquarters at extension 2304.

Medical Services

First aid is available at park headquarters, visitor centers, and ranger stations. Hospitals are located in Morton, Enumclaw, and Puyallup.

Pets

Pets are permitted on leashes on the West Side Road, Sunrise Pet Walk, parking lots, campgrounds, and paved roads, but are not permitted on trails or in public buildings. Kennels are available in Eatonville. Leashes may not exceed six feet.

Safety and Regulations

For your safety and enjoyment and for the protection of the park, please follow these regulations and suggestions:

- Fires are permitted only in established rings or grills at picnic areas and campgrounds. Portable stoves must be used in the backcountry for cooking. Gathering of firewood is prohibited.

- In the subalpine meadows, hikers are urged to remain on designated trails and avoid trampling the fragile plantlife.

- Mountain climbers are encouraged to wear hard hats because of the risk of falling rocks and ice and to climb with established guide services, such as Rainier Mountaineering, Inc. (available at 360-569-2227 in summer and 206-627-6242 in winter).

- Visitors should be prepared for sudden weather changes. Avalanches, in particular, can pose a risk to climbers, especially in late spring and early summer.

- Persons with heart or respiratory difficulties should be careful to avoid overexertion, especially at higher elevations.

- Feeding, disturbing, capturing, or hunting wildlife and damaging plantlife is prohibited.

The National Park Service asks that visitors not litter the park. Remember the excellent slogan to "leave only footprints" as a guide to help protect this national park.

ACTIVITIES

Hiking, mountain climbing, birdwatching, picnicking, camping, horseback riding, non-motorized boating on some lakes, fishing (no

license required), interpreter-led walks, evening campfire programs, field seminars, children's programs, bus tours, cross-country skiing, snowshoeing, and sledding. Further information is provided in the park's *Tahoma News* newspaper.

Hiking Trails

Among the more than 300 miles of trails are the following:

In the Longmire vicinity: **Historic Longmire Walking Tour**, an easy 1.25-mile, round-trip, self-guided interpretive walk that presents some impressive, rustic structures, including the National Park Inn, general store, museum, park headquarters, library, and Nisqually Bridge; **Trail of the Shadows**, an easy half-mile, self-guided interpretive loop around Longmire Meadow, beginning across the main road from the National Park Inn, and including a historic log cabin that is the park's oldest structure; **Carter Falls Trail**, an easy, one-mile route beginning 100 yards downhill from the entrance of Cougar Rock Campground, following along Paradise River in a lush, old-growth conifer forest, and ending at this beautiful waterfall. Madcap Falls is another 50 yards beyond; **Eagle Peak Trail**, a strenuous, 3.5-mile, 2,955-foot climb, beginning 50 yards beyond the Nisqually River Suspension Bridge and proceeding through lush, old-growth forest. The trail affords exciting views of Mount Rainier, Nisqually Valley, and the jagged peaks of the Tatoosh Range; and **Wonderland Trail to Paradise**, a partly moderate and partly strenuous, 6-mile, 2,700-foot climb beginning near the Wilderness Information Center (Hiker Center); proceeding along the Nisqually River, in lush, old-growth forest; passing Carter, Madcap, and Narada falls; and climbing steeply into the subalpine fir-dotted meadows around Paradise.

In the Paradise vicinity (in this area, the National Park Service urges hikers to *stay on designated trails*, as walking on the subalpine meadows damages and may even kill the fragile plantlife): **Nisqually Vista Trail**, an easy 1.2-mile, self-guiding interpretive loop beginning and ending at the Jackson Memorial Visitor Center. The trail provides grand views of Mount Rainier, Nisqually Glacier, and summer wildflowers blooming in the fir-framed subalpine meadows; **Alta Vista Trail**, an easy 1.5-mile loop trail beginning and ending at the Jackson Memorial Visitor Center and providing opportunities to see summer wildflowers and a view overlooking Paradise River; **Lakes Trail**, a moderately strenuous, 5-mile loop beginning and ending at the Jackson Memorial Visitor Center, proceeding through subalpine meadows dotted with clumps of subalpine firs, passing the Reflection Lakes, and providing views of Mount Rainier and the jagged peaks of the Tatoosh Range; and **Skyline Trail**, a moderately strenuous, 5-mile loop beginning and ending at the Jackson Memorial Visitor Center, passing through meadows filled with summer wildflowers and framed by subalpine firs, and leading above timberline for views of Nisqually Glacier, Mount St. Helens, and Mount Adams.

In the Ohanapecosh vicinity: **Ohanapecosh Hot Springs Trail**, an easy, half-mile, self-guided interpretive loop walk beginning and ending behind Ohanapecosh Visitor Center, leading through a forest of towering Douglas firs and hemlocks to Ohanapecosh Hot Springs; **Silver Falls Trail**, an easy 3-mile loop beginning and ending at Ohanapecosh Campground's Loop B, proceeding through old-growth forest along the Ohanapecosh River, and providing a view of beautiful, 75-foot-high Silver Falls; and **Grove of the Patriarchs Trail**, an easy 1.3-mile, self-guided interpretive loop beginning and ending near the Stevens Canyon Entrance Station, crossing to a large island in the Ohanapecosh River, and leading through a magnificent stand of giant, old-growth Douglas firs, western redcedars, and western hemlocks—some of which are believed to be at least 1,000 years old.

In the Tipsoo Lake vicinity: **Naches Peak Trail**, a moderately easy, 3.5-mile loop beginning and ending at the park's Chinook Pass entrance, passing by Tipsoo Lake, from which there is a magnificent view of Mount Rainier, and looping around the east side of Naches Peak, on a short stretch of the Pacific Crest National Scenic Trail in the Wenatchee National Forest's William O. Douglas Wilderness.

In the Sunrise vicinity (in this area, the National Park Service urges hikers to *stay on designated trails*, as walking on the subalpine meadows damages and may even kill the fragile plantlife): **Emmons Vista Trail**, an easy quarter-mile route, beginning at the Sunrise Visitor Center and providing breathtaking views of Mount Rainier and the Emmons Glacier; **Sourdough Ridge Trail**, an easy 1.5-mile, self-guided interpretive loop beginning and ending at the Sunrise Visitor Center and providing grand views of Mount Rainier from meadows framed with subalpine firs and abloom with summer wildflowers; **Sunrise Rim Trail**, an easy 3-mile loop beginning at the Sunrise Visitor Center and providing magnificent views of Mount Rainier and the Emmons Glacier; and **Sunrise-Frozen Lake-Shadow Lake Trail**, a moderately strenuous, 5-mile loop beginning and ending at the Sunrise Visitor Center and providing great views of Mount Rainier, the Emmons Glacier, Frozen and Shadow lakes, and subalpine meadows ablaze with the colors of summer wildflowers.

In the Carbon River vicinity: **Carbon River Rain Forest Trail**, an easy .3-mile, self-guided interpretive loop beginning and ending at the Carbon River Ranger Station and winding through the park's only true inland rainforest, with enormous Sitka spruces, Douglas firs, and western red cedars; and **Carbon Glacier Trail**, a moderately strenuous, 3.4-mile route beginning at Ipsut Creek Campground (at the end of Carbon River Road), proceeding through lush, old-growth rainforest along the Carbon River, and reaching the end of Carbon Glacier. The National Park Service cautions hikers, "Beware of falling rocks from the glacier snout."

Encircling Mount Rainier: **Wonderland Trail**, a challenging, 93-mile route that encircles Mount Rainier, providing awesome views of the mountain and passing through a variety of the park's diverse ecosystems—from lush, lowland conifer forests to subalpine fir-framed meadows filled with colorful summer wildflowers. Visitors planning to hike part or all of this trail should contact the National Park Service for information and advice regarding wilderness regulations, campsites, and weather and trail conditions. Backcountry permits are

required and can be obtained at wilderness information centers.

Lodging and Dining

Reservations (as far in advance as possible) can be made for the following lodging accommodations by contacting Mount Rainier Guest Services, Inc., P.O. Box 108, Ashford, WA 98304; 206-569-2275:

Paradise Inn, a rustic hotel dating from 1917, open from late-May to early October, providing rooms, dining room, elegant great hall, snack bar, cocktail lounge, and gift shop.

National Park Inn, a small, historic hotel at Longmire, open year-round, offering rooms (some without private bath) and a restaurant.

A grill is located at the Paradise visitor center.

Lodging Outside the Park

Accommodations are available in such nearby communities as Ashford, Eatonville, Packwood, Morton, Rimrock, and Enumclaw, as well as such cities as Seattle, Tacoma, and Yakima. Please consider using them to decrease visitor impact on the park.

Campgrounds

All but one of the park's campgrounds are open from June through September or longer, depending on the weather and elevation; Sunshine Point Campground is open year-round. Reservations can be made for sites at Ohanapecosh and Cougar Rock campgrounds during the period July 1 through Labor Day by calling the National Park Reservation Service at 800-365-CAMP. At other times and at the other campgrounds, individual sites are on a first-come, first-served basis. Reservations for group camping are required and accepted up to 90 days in advance; they may be made by calling the park.

51

◀ *Mountain ash in Mount Rainier National Park, Washington*

Backcountry Camping

Wilderness camping is allowed year-round throughout much of the park on a first-come, first-served basis. Permits are required and are issued at visitor centers, wilderness information centers, and ranger stations. Fires are not permitted in the backcountry, so a portable camp stove is needed for cooking.

FLORA AND FAUNA (Partial Listings)

Mammals: mountain goat, Roosevelt elk, black-tailed (mule) deer, black bear, mountain lion, bobcat, coyote, red fox, pine marten, fisher, mink, longtail and shorttail weasels, hoary marmot, beaver, mountain beaver, porcupine, raccoon, striped and spotted skunks, snowshoe hare, pika, chickaree, golden-mantled squirrel, and Townsend and yellow pine chipmunks.

Birds: spotted sandpiper, blue grouse, white-tailed ptarmigan, red-tailed hawk, golden eagle, western screech and great horned owls, belted kingfisher, band-tailed pigeon, rufous hummingbird, pileated and hairy woodpeckers, flicker, olive-sided and Pacific-slope (western) flycatchers, Vaux's swift, violet-green and barn swallows, raven, Steller's and gray jays, Clark's nutcracker, mountain and chestnut-backed chickadees, red-breasted nuthatch, brown creeper, winter wren, dipper, ruby-crowned and golden-crowned kinglets, robin, thrushes (varied, Swainson's, and hermit), Townsend's solitaire, American pipit, warblers (yellow-rumped, Townsend's, MacGillivray's, yellow, orange-crowned, and Wilson's), western tanager, sparrows (golden-crowned, chipping, fox, song, and Lincoln's), dark-eyed junco, gray-crowned rosy finch, Cassin's finch, red crossbill, and pine siskin.

Trees, Shrubs, and Flowers: pines (western white, whitebark, lodgepole, and ponderosa), Sitka and Engelmann spruces, western and mountain hemlocks, Douglas fir, firs (subalpine, grand or lowland, silver, and noble), western red cedar, Alaska (yellow) cedar, Pacific yew, black cottonwood, red alder, Pacific madrone, mountain-ash, Pacific dogwood, maples (bigleaf, western mountain, and vine), salal, salmonberry, thimbleberry, huckleberry, blueberry, Cascade azalea, heathers (white, red, and yellow), bearberry (kinnikinnick), false hellebore, devil's club, beargrass, fireweed, lilies (Columbia tiger, glacier, and avalanche), shootingstar, monkshood, larkspur, pleated gentian, blue lupine, yellow monkeyflower, red columbine, skunk cabbage, magenta and scarlet paintbrushes, coral-root, bog and calypso orchids, starflower, oxalis, spring beauty, false Solomon's-seal, bunchberry, Pacific trillium, cliff and Davidson penstemons, silky phacelia, purple and yellow violets, twinflower, bluebell, Mertensia, sandwort, mountain bistort, Lyell rock cress, phlox, stonecrop, moss campion, western pasqueflower, elephant-head, and subalpine buttercup. There are also numerous varieties of ferns, mosses, liverworts, and fungi, especially in the lush lowland forests of the western part of the park.

NEARBY POINTS OF INTEREST

The areas surrounding Mount Rainier National Park offer numerous fascinating attractions that can be enjoyed as day trips or overnight excursions. Mt. Baker-Snoqualmie, Gifford Pinchot, and Wenatchee national forests adjoin the park. North Cascades National Park is to the north; Olympic National Park and Ebey's Landing National Historical Reserve are to the northwest; and Fort Vancouver National Historic Site and the U.S. Forest Service-managed Mount St. Helens National Volcanic Monument are to the southwest.

NORTH CASCADES NATIONAL PARK

▲ *Baker River Rainforest*

North Cascades National Park

2105 State Route 20
Sedro Woolley, WA 98284-9314
360-856-5700

This two-unit, 504,781-acre national park at the north end of the Cascade Mountains in north-central Washington state protects awesomely rugged and stunningly scenic wilderness country. It includes jagged, glacier-covered peaks; deep, glacier-carved valleys; sparkling subalpine lakes; dashing streams and rivers; plunging cascades and waterfalls; and ecologically rich forests. More than 300 glaciers—over half of all the glaciers in the lower 48 states—are located there. The rich biological diversity of the park provides for a profusion of flora and fauna: more than 1,500 varieties of plantlife and hundreds of animal species. Early autumn brings bright splashes of color to the foliage of larch, maple, dogwood, cottonwood, and alder, contrasting with the predominant evergreen conifers. For wilderness enthusiasts, the park offers a wealth of hiking and mountaineering opportunities.

The year 1892 was the first time advocates made the case for protecting this fabulously scenic area as a national park. In 1897, it was included within the Washington Forest Reserve, which was subsequently divided among three national forests. But over the next half-century, such environmental organizations as The Mountaineers, Sierra Club, The Wilderness Society, and NPCA expressed concern that the U.S. Forest Service was failing to adequately protect the area. As the result of nationwide public pressure, a joint National Park Service-Forest Service study of the North Cascades was undertaken. In 1965, the study team released its recommendations, calling special attention to the distinctiveness of the area: "The portion of the North Cascades in the Study Area defies description. Here occurs the most breathtakingly beautiful and spectacular mountain scenery in the 48 contiguous States. . . . particularly the Eldorado Peaks complex, the Picket Range and Mount Shuksan are what have been termed the 'American Alps.' Here is scenic grandeur that unquestionably belongs in our national gallery of natural beauty." In 1968, the park was established, and two years later most of the park was designated as wilderness—part of the 634,614-acre Stephen Mather Wilderness extending into the adjacent Lake Chelan and Ross Lake national recreation areas. (See also the separate entries on those recreation areas.)

Conservationists in the United States and Canada, including NPCA, have long supported a proposal for a North Cascades *International* Park. The area included in such an expanded park would encompass worthy parts of British Columbia's adjacent Manning and Cathedral provincial parks.

OUTSTANDING FEATURES

Among outstanding features in the *South Unit* of the park are: **Stehekin Valley**, a glacier-carved, richly forested valley into which the rushing Stehekin River Stehekin is an Indian word meaning "the way through"descends from Cascade Pass, is joined by numerous tributaries in the park and farther down in the Lake Chelan National Recreation Area, flows into the upper end of Lake Chelan ; and the **Eldorado Peaks**, a complex of extensive glaciers, snowfields, and magnificent summits, the highest rising to 8,672 feet above sea level atop Eldorado Peak.

In the *North Unit*, outstanding features include: **Picket Range**, a jumble of sheer-faced, rocky spires and peaks, thrusting above 8,200 feet elevation, including Mount Fury, Mount Challenger, and Luna Peak—the latter known as the Matterhorn of the "American Alps"; **Big Beaver** and **Little Beaver valleys**, two lushly forested valleys with dashing streams that descend from the high mountains, through the park and Ross Lake National Recreation Area, to the shore of the lake; and **Mount Shuksan**, an awesome mass of a mountain that at 9,131 feet is the park's highest. One of the best views of this mountain is from Picture Lake, along the Mount Baker Ski Area road (State Route 542), in Mount Baker-Snoqualmie National Forest.

NORTH CASCADES NATIONAL PARK

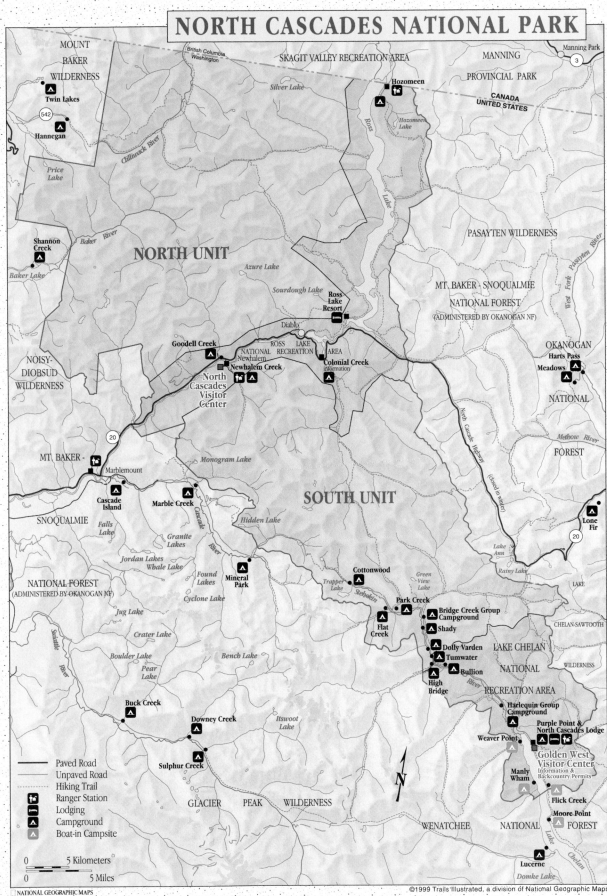

MOUNT BAKER WILDERNESS

Twin Lakes

542

Hannegan

Price Lake

Shannon Creek

Baker Lake

Baker River

NORTH UNIT

Azure Lake

Sourdough Lake

Silver Lake

Ross Lake

SKAGIT VALLEY RECREATION AREA

British Columbia / Washington

Hozomeen

Hozomeen Lake

MANNING

PROVINCIAL PARK

Manning Park

3

CANADA
UNITED STATES

PASAYTEN WILDERNESS

MT. BAKER - SNOQUALMIE

NATIONAL FOREST

(ADMINISTERED BY OKANOGAN NF)

Ross Lake Resort

Diablo

Goodell Creek

NATIONAL ROSS LAKE RECREATION

Newhalem

Newhalem Creek

North Cascades Visitor Center

AREA

Colonial Creek information

NOISY-DIOBSUD WILDERNESS

20

MT. BAKER - SNOQUALMIE

Marblemount

Cascade Island

Marble Creek

NATIONAL FOREST

(ADMINISTERED BY OKANOGAN NF)

Falls Lake

Granite Lakes

Jordan Lakes
Whale Lake

Found Lakes

Cyclone Lake

Jug Lake

Crater Lake

Boulder Lake

Pear Lake

Monogram Lake

Hidden Lake

Cascade River

Mineral Park

Bench Lake

SOUTH UNIT

OKANOGAN

Harts Pass
Meadows

NATIONAL

FOREST

Methow River

North Cascade Highway

(closed in winter)

Lake Ann

Rainy Lake

20

Lone Fir

LAKE

CHELAN-SAWTOOTH

LAKE CHELAN

NATIONAL

WILDERNESS

RECREATION AREA

Trapper Lake

Cottonwood

Green View Lake

Stehekin

Park Creek

Bridge Creek Group Campground

Shady

Flat Creek

Dolly Varden

Tumwater

Bullion

High Bridge

Stehekin River

Harlequin Group Campground

Purple Point & North Cascades Lodge

Weaver Point

Golden West Visitor Center
Information & Backcountry Permits

Manly Wham

Flick Creek

Moore Point

Buck Creek

Suiattle River

Downey Creek

Itswoot Lake

Sulphur Creek

GLACIER PEAK WILDERNESS

N

WENATCHEE

NATIONAL

FOREST

Lucerne

Domke Lake

Lake Chelan

Legend

——— Paved Road

——— Unpaved Road

········· Hiking Trail

Ranger Station

Lodging

Campground

Boat-in Campsite

0   5 Kilometers

0   5 Miles

NATIONAL GEOGRAPHIC MAPS
TRAILS ILLUSTRATED

©1999 Trails Illustrated, a division of National Geographic Maps.

▲ *Mount Shuksan in the North Cascades National Park, Washington*

When to Go

The park is open year-round, but snow limits backcountry access. Lower elevation trails are normally free of snow from April to mid-October; higher elevation trails may have snow until mid-July. On the west side of the Cascades, rainfall is greater and skies are often cloudy, while there is usually less rainfall and more sunshine on the east side.

How to Get There

By Car/Boat/Float Plane: From I-5 at Burlington, drive east about 50 miles on State Route 20 to Ross Lake National Recreation Area (NRA), from which there are numerous trails leading from the recreation area into both the North and South units of the park. From U.S. Route 97 near Pateros, drive northwest 31 miles on State Route 153 and then northwest about 70 miles on State Route 20, to Ross Lake NRA. Visitors to the southern part of the park's South Unit arrive either by boat (daily service is provided from Chelan to Stehekin from mid-March to the end of October by Lake Chelan Boat Company, Chelan, WA 98816; 509-682-2224) or by float plane (service provided by Chelan Airways, Chelan, WA 98816; 509-682-5555). From Stehekin, trails lead through Lake Chelan NRA and into the park. From mid-May to mid-October, a daily shuttle service makes regular runs on the Stehekin Valley road that leads into the park; a fee is charged for the shuttle, and reservations are required (call 360-856-5700, ext. 340 or 14).

By Air: Seattle-Tacoma International Airport (260-431-4444), Bellingham International Airport (360-676-2500), and Spokane Airport are served by major airlines. Chelan Airways provides float-plane service between Chelan and Stehekin (see above).

By Train: Amtrak (800-872-7245) stops in Seattle, Everett, and Wenatchee.

By Bus: Greyhound Lines (800-231-2222) stops in Seattle, Everett, and Wenatchee.

Fees and Permits

There is no entrance fee. Free backcountry camping permits are required and can be obtained at park offices, ranger stations, and North Cascades and Golden West visitor centers. Fishing requires a state license, and permits are required for stock use. While hunting is prohibited within the North Cascades National Park, it is allowed during the designated season in parts of the two national recreation areas.

Visitor and Information Centers

North Cascades Visitor Center, in Ross Lake National Recreation Area just south of State Route 20: open daily from May through October and weekends in winter. Interpretive programs, publications, maps, and backcountry permits.

Golden West Visitor Center, at Stehekin in Lake Chelan National Recreation Area: open Memorial Day thru Columbus Day. Information, publications, maps, and backcountry permits. For information, call 360-856-5700, ext. 340, and then ext. 14.

Park Headquarters, at Sedro Woolley six miles east of I-5 on State Route 20: open weekdays year-round and summer weekends. Information, publications, maps, and backcountry permits.

Wilderness Information Center, located at Marblemount, just off State Route 20. For information, call 360-873-4500, ext. 39. Heather Meadows Visitor Center, near the end of the Mount Baker Ski Area road in Mount Baker-Snoqualmie National Forest: open daily July to mid-September. Interpretive information, publications, maps, and backcountry permits.

Facilities

Lodging, restaurant, shuttle bus service, campgrounds, hot showers, laundry, boat launch ramps, professional guide service, post office, and camp store.

Handicapped Accessibility

Trails that are wheelchair accessible are Shadow of the Sentinels, Sterling Munro, Happy Creek Forest Walk, Picture Lake Path,

57

59

▲ *Nooksack Falls in North Cascades National Park, Washington*

▲ Mount Shuksan in North Cascades National Park, Washington

Trail of the Cedars, Rainy Lake Trail, sections of Fire and Ice, and Artist Ridge. Accessible visitor centers are North Cascades in Ross Lake NRA, Golden West at Stehekin in Lake Chelan NRA, Heather Meadows in Mount Baker-Snoqualmie National Forest, Wilderness Information Station at Marblemount, and park headquarters in Sedro Woolley. There are accessible campgrounds in Ross Lake National Recreation Area (NRA) at Goodell Creek, Newhalem Creek, and Colonial Creek.

Medical Services

First aid is available at visitor centers and ranger stations. The nearest hospitals are in Sedro Woolley and Chelan.

Pets

Pets are not permitted in the national park, except on leashes on the Pacific Crest Trail and in the surrounding national forests and NRAs. In Mount Baker-Snoqalmie National Forest, pets are prohibited on Picture Lake Path and Table Mountain Trail, both at Heather Meadows.

Safety and Regulations

For your safety and enjoyment and for the protection of the park, please follow these regulations and suggestions:

- Fires are permitted only in authorized locations; only dead and down wood may be used for fuel.

- Water in the backcountry must be treated, filtered, or boiled.

- Campers are urged to practice minimum-impact camping and bear-country camping procedures. For important tips on hiking and camping safely in bear country, ask for a copy of the National Park Service's *Bears and You in the North Cascades.*

- Waters are often not conducive to swimming because of frigid temperatures.

- Since weather conditions can change rapidly, hikers and campers should check with a ranger for detailed information on weather and trail conditions, and carry appropriate clothing and supplies. During heavy spring runoff, hikers should be especially careful of

swift and powerful currents of streams and rivers.

- Feeding, disturbing, capturing, or hunting wildlife and damaging plantlife are prohibited in the national park.

The National Park Service asks that visitors not litter the park. Remember the excellent slogan to "leave only footprints" as a guide to help protect this national park.

ACTIVITIES

Hiking, bicycling (rentals available), mountain climbing, technical rock climbing, birdwatching, picnicking, camping, river rafting, horse and mule rentals, and boating (rentals available). Further information is provided in the North Cascades National Park–Mt. Baker-Snoqualmie National Forest visitor information guide, *North Cascades Challenger.*

Hiking Trails

Among the more than 350 miles of trails in North Cascades National Park and adjacent national recreation areas are the following:

In the Stehekin Valley vicinity: **Imus Creek Trail**, an easy .75-mile, self-guided interpretive walk in Lake Chelan NRA, beginning at the Golden West Visitor Center; **Chelan Lakeshore Trail**, a fairly level route in Lake Chelan NRA, beginning near the Golden West Visitor Center and leading to such places as a waterfall on Hazard Creek in a half-mile, Fourmile Creek in just over two miles, and Flick Creek Camp in 3.6 miles; **Stehekin River Trail**, a fairly easy, four-mile route in Lake Chelan NRA, beginning at Harlequin Campground (shuttle service from Golden West Visitor Center to Harlequin, from mid-May to mid-October), descending through the lush valley-bottom forest, providing occasional views of Stehekin River, crossing a number of tributaries on footbridges, and ending at Weaver Point, on Lake Chelan. Hikers may arrange with North Cascades Lodge to be transported by boat from Weaver Point to Stehekin; **Rainbow Falls Trail**, an easy 100-yard walk in Lake Chelan NRA, beginning at the end of the Rainbow Falls spur road that branches from the Stehekin Valley Road (shuttle route) and ending at the base of this 312-foot waterfall, the volume of which varies greatly from spring to autumn. A picnic area is located nearby; **Rainbow Loop Trail**, a moderately strenuous, 4.6-mile route in Lake Chelan NRA, running between the upper trailhead (five miles up the Stehekin River Road from Stehekin Landing) and the lower trailhead (three miles up the Stehekin River Road). Both trailheads are on the mid-May to mid-October shuttle route; **Agnes Gorge Trail**, a fairly easy, 2.5-mile route on a stretch of the Pacific Crest National Scenic Trail, beginning at High Bridge (served by the mid-May to mid-October shuttle) at the North Cascades NP-Lake Chelan NRA boundary, proceeding through the NRA, crossing into Wenatchee National Forest's Glacier Peak Wilderness, and affording views of Agnes Creek's waterfalls and gorge; **Cascade Pass Trail**, a strenuous, five-mile, 2,650-foot climb in North Cascades National Park, beginning at Cottonwood Campground at the end of the Stehekin Valley Road and reaching this 5,384-foot-high elevation. Cascade Pass can also be reached by hiking four miles from the end of the Cascade River Road from Marblemount.

In the Ross Lake National Recreation Area vicinity: **River Trail**, an easy one-mile loop, beginning and ending at Newhalem Campground (just off State Route 20) and winding through a beautiful area of lush, old-growth forest along the Skagit River; **Pyramid Lake Trail**, a fairly strenuous, two-mile, 1,500-foot climb in Ross Lake NRA, beginning at milepost 127 on State Route 20 (near Diablo), following a stream through lush forest, and reaching this beautiful little lake; **Thunder Creek Trail**, the lower part of which is an easy 1.5-mile route in Ross Lake NRA, beginning at Colonial Creek Campground (just off State Route 20), following the shore of Diablo Lake, crossing a suspension bridge near the mouth of Thunder Creek, proceeding through a lush, old-growth conifer forest, and reaching Thunder Camp on a short spur trail. For longer treks, Thunder Creek Trail continues as a much more strenuous

▶ *Baker River Rainforest in North Cascades National Park, Washington*

climb, providing some exciting mountain views from along Fisher Creek and topping out at 6,063-foot Park Creek Pass (19 miles from Colonial Creek Campground) in the heart of North Cascades National Park's South Unit. From this pass, Park Creek Trail descends seven miles to Park Creek Campground, on the Stehekin Valley Road; and **Big Beaver Trail**, which provides a variety of hiking opportunities beginning at Ross Dam, passing Ross Lake Resort, and continuing along the west shore of Ross Lake to the mouth of Big Beaver Creek. From there, this route proceeds beneath giant western redcedars and follows this stream for

OVERNIGHT STAYS

Lodging and Dining

Lodging facilities are not available within park boundaries; however, Ross Lake and Lake Chelan national recreation areas offer the following accommodations:

Ross Lake Resort (206-386-4437), open from late June through October, providing cabins.

North Cascades Stehekin Lodge (509-682-4494) at Stehekin, on Lake Chelan, providing rooms and meals year-round.

Lodging Outside the Park

Accommodations are available in nearby communities such as Sedro Woolley, Concrete, Rockport, Marblemount, Mazama, Winthrop, Twisp, Chelan, and Manson.

Campgrounds

Goodell Creek, Newhalem Creek, and Colonial Creek campgrounds are located just off State Route 20 in Ross Lake National Recreation Area. Hozomeen Campground is located near the north end of Ross Lake, reached on the Silver-Skagit Road from Hope, British Columbia. Purple Point Campground is on the shore of Lake Chelan, and Bullion is by the Stehekin River, both in the Lake Chelan National Recreation Area. Seven campgrounds are located farther up Stehekin Valley in the park. Sites in these campgrounds are taken on a first-come, first-served basis. Two group campgrounds, requiring reservations, are located in Stehekin Valley. To avoid attracting bears, campers are urged to practice minimum-impact camping, keep a clean campsite, and store food appropriately.

Backcountry Camping

Camping is allowed year-round throughout most of the park backcountry on a first-come, first-served basis. Permits are required. Sites can be reached by hiking and boating and on

65

roughly ten miles (crossing into North Cascade National Park's North Unit in about five miles). When it reaches 3,619-foot Beaver Pass, it descends to Little Beaver Trail, which leads eastward to Ross Lake or west to 5,218-foot Whatcom Pass, and connects with Brush Creek Trail and then Hannegan Trail.

horseback. Organized groups of up to 12 people may camp along Ross Lake at Boundary Bay, Green Point, McMillan, Ponderosa, and Silver Creek. Where stock is permitted, groups are limited to 12 pairs of eyes (includes humans and animals). Other party limits are six people per site.

FLORA AND FAUNA (Partial Listings)

Mammals: mountain goat, blacktail (mule) deer, grizzly and black bears, mountain lion, lynx, bobcat, gray wolf, coyote, red fox, wolverine, fisher, pine marten, shorttail and longtail weasels, river otter, porcupine, raccoon, striped skunk, beaver, hoary marmot, snowshoe hare, cottontail, pika, golden-mantled squirrel, chickaree, and Townsend and yellow pine chipmunks.

Birds: common loon, mallard, bufflehead, common and Barrow's goldeneyes, harlequin duck, common merganser, great blue heron, killdeer, spotted sandpiper, ruffed and blue grouse, white-tailed ptarmigan, hawks (sharp-shinned, Cooper's, and red-tailed), northern goshawk, bald and golden eagles, osprey, owls (barred, great horned, spotted, and northern-pygmy), belted kingfisher, band-tailed pigeon, rufous hummingbird, woodpeckers (pileated, downy, and hairy), flicker, red-breasted sapsucker, flycatchers (olive-sided, willow, Hammond's, dusky, and Pacific-slope or western), American pipit, Vaux's swift, swallows (tree, northern rough-winged, violet-green, cliff, and barn), crow, raven, Steller's and gray jays, Clark's nutcracker, chickadees (mountain, black-capped, and chestnut-backed), red-breasted nuthatch, brown creeper, winter wren, dipper, golden-crowned kinglet, robin, varied and Swainson's thrushes, Townsend's solitaire, mountain bluebird, cedar waxwing, warbling vireo, warblers (yellow-rumped, Townsend's, yellow, and yellowthroat), western tanager, sparrows (white-crowned,

chipping, fox, and song), dark-eyed junco, gray-crowned rosy finch, red crossbill, Cassin's finch, and pine siskin.

Trees, Shrubs, and Flowers: pines (western white, whitebark, lodgepole, and ponderosa), firs (Douglas, silver, grand, and subalpine), Sitka and Engelmann spruces, western larch, mountain and western hemlocks, western redcedar, Alaska (yellow) cedar, western yew, black cottonwood, quaking aspen, willow, red and Sitka alders, black and Northwestern paper birches, California hazel, maples (vine, Rocky Mountain, and bigleaf), Pacific and red osier dogwoods, salmonberry, thimbleberry, huckleberry, mountain heather, prickly currant, salal, false hellebore, fireweed, cow parsnip, Oregon grape, partridge foot, bunchberry, glacier and avalanche lilies, calypso orchid, bleedingheart, red columbine, fanleaf cinquefoil, paintbrush, western anemone, lupine, red and yellow monkeyflowers, shootingstar, monkshood, pleated gentian, penstemon, Sitka valerian, sky pilot, foamflower, trillium, twinflower, yellow violet, Tolmie's saxifrage, and alpine phlox.

NEARBY POINTS OF INTEREST

The areas surrounding North Cascades National Park offer some exceptional attractions that can be enjoyed as day trips or overnight excursions. Okanogan, Wenatchee, and Mount Baker-Snoqualmie national forests adjoin the national park and recreation areas. Ebey's Landing National Historical Reserve and San Juan Island National Historical Park are to the west, in Puget Sound; and Olympic National Park is to the southwest, on the Olympic Peninsula. Mount Rainier National Park is to the south. Lake Roosevelt National Recreation Area, behind Grand Coulee Dam, is to the east. Manning and Cathedral provincial parks border the park to the north, in British Columbia, Canada.

Olympic National Park

▲ *Moss-covered trees in Queets Valley*

OLYMPIC NATIONAL PARK

600 East Park Avenue
Port Angeles, WA 98362
360-452-4501

This three-unit, 922,651-acre national park on the Olympic Peninsula of northwest Washington state protects one of the most biologically rich areas in North America. The park's incredible scenic diversity includes the rugged, surf-pounded, 60-mile Pacific Ocean coastal strip, containing fortress-like seastacks and islands, headlands and bluffs, strands of beach, and stretches of rocky shore where tidepools are filled with delicate intertidal life. Inland, between the coast and the Olympic Mountains, rivers flow through valleys of luxuriant primeval rainforest, consisting of gigantic Sitka spruces, Douglas firs, western redcedars, and western hemlocks, with an understory of maples. Thickly carpeting this hushed world of greenery, which receives around 140 inches of precipitation annually, is the lushness of ferns, clubmosses, mosses, lichens, fungi, and other shade-tolerant, moisture-loving plantlife. Higher in the richly forested valleys of the Olympic Mountains are countless rushing streams and plunging waterfalls. Higher still, exquisite, jewel-like mountain lakes occupy small glacier-carved basins, and fir-framed, subalpine meadows are decked out with pageants of colorful summer wildflowers. Above it all, vast snowfields and massive tongues of glacial ice drape the heights of the Olympic Mountains—crowned by massive 7,965-foot-high Mount Olympus.

Annual precipitation on the Olympic Peninsula varies dramatically from around 150 to 200 inches in the western part of the mountains (the highest precipitation in the lower 48 states), to only 17 inches in the "rain shadow" just east of the mountains. These great mountains effectively "capture" most of the precipitation that storms bring off the Pacific Ocean. More than 1,200 kinds of plantlife, 200 species of birds, and 70 varieties of mammals are known to inhabit the park's rich wilderness habitats.

A presidential proclamation in 1909 initially established the area as Mount Olympus National Monument. In 1933, it was transferred from the U.S. Forest Service to the National Park Service, and, in 1938, it was made a national park. In 1976, the area was named a Biosphere Reserve and, in 1981, a World Heritage Site. In 1988, most of the park was designated as wilderness.

OUTSTANDING FEATURES

Among the many outstanding features of the park are the following: **Hoh Rain Forest**, a lush green, primeval valley accessible by road and trail along the Hoh River, where towering trees and rich carpets of mosses and ferns dominate; **Queets Rain Forest**, a second lush rainforest valley, accessible by road and trail, where the park's largest-known Douglas fir grows; **Quinault Rain Forest**, a third lush rainforest valley, accessible by road and trail; **Lake Crescent**, the largest freshwater body of water in the park; **Marymere Falls**, a spectacular 90-foot waterfall, reached by a short trail just a mile south of Crescent Lake; **Sol Duc Hot Springs**, a resort where natural water temperatures range from lukewarm to 138 degrees; **Sol Duc Falls**, a beautiful waterfall plunging into a small gorge amid a rich lowland forest; **Seven Lakes Basin**, a beautiful area of small mountain lakes in the upper Sol Duc River watershed; **Hurricane Ridge**, a perfect spot for viewing the breathtaking panorama of snow-clad peaks of the Olympic Mountains; **Mount Olympus**, the central, massive, glacier-draped core of the Olympic Mountains, with a number of jagged peaks rising to just under 8,000 feet above sea level; **Blue Glacier**, at three miles long and 900 feet thick, one of six major glaciers on Mount Olympus; and the **Pacific coastal strip**, 60 miles of wild, surf-pounded beaches, rocky shore with tidepools, and sheer headlands and bluffs, with seastacks and islands just offshore.

PRACTICAL INFORMATION

When to Go

The park is open year-round, but roads at higher elevations may be closed in winter. The climate is characterized by extreme unpredictabili-

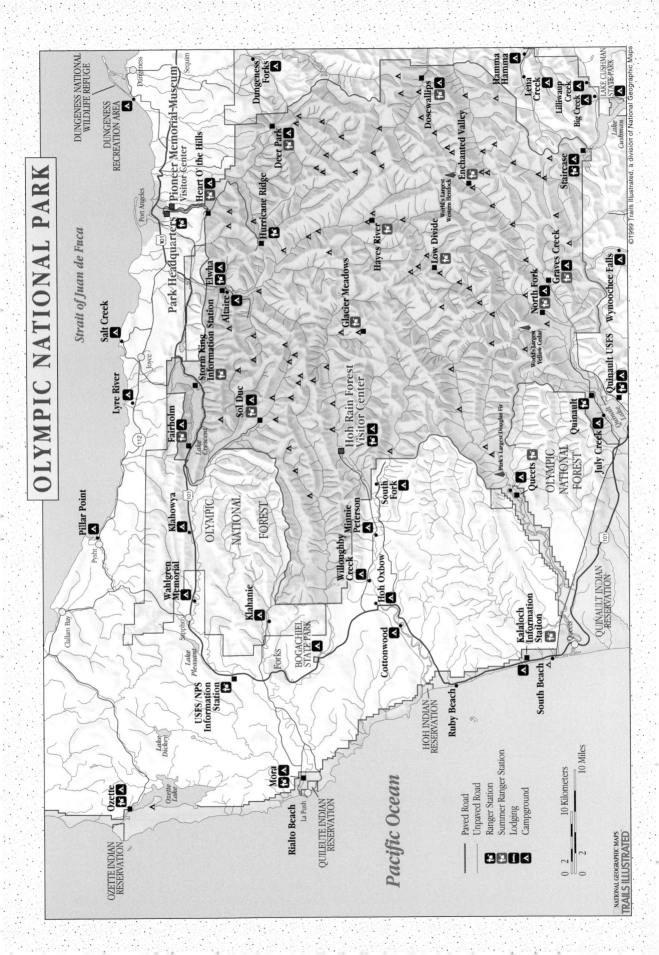

OLYMPIC NATIONAL PARK

Strait of Juan de Fuca

Pacific Ocean

NATIONAL GEOGRAPHIC MAPS
TRAILS ILLUSTRATED

©1999 Trails Illustrated, a division of National Geographic Maps

Legend
- Paved Road
- Unpaved Road
- Ranger Station
- Summer Ranger Station
- Lodging
- Campground

0   2   10 Kilometers
0   2   10 Miles

▲ *Lupine and Mount Olympus in Olympic National Park, Washington*

ty and varied rainfall. The park's western side is very wet, while the northeast is very dry. Winter temperatures are in the 40s, with snowfall light at lower elevations. Spring is mostly wet, mild, and windy, and temperatures vary from 35 to 60 degrees. Summer is predominantly fair and warm, from about 66 to 80 degrees, with coastal fog later in the season. Fall is usually cool and wet with occasional winds and possible early snow in the mountains; temperatures range from 35 to 65 degrees.

How to Get There

By Car: From I-5 at Tacoma, drive north 26 miles on State Route 16, north 26 miles on State Route 3, northwest 16 miles on State Route 104, and west 37 miles on U.S. Route 101, to Port Angeles, where the park's main visitor center and start of the road up to Hurricane Ridge are located. From Port Angeles, there are six different route possibilities, depending on the section of the park you want to enter. One possibility is to drive west about 15 miles to where U.S. 101 enters a stretch of the park along the shore of Crescent Lake. A second is to drive west 28 miles on U.S. 101 to where the Sol Duc Road branches to the southeast into the park. A third is to drive west and south about 70 miles on U.S. 101 to where the Hoh Rain Forest Road branches east. A fourth is to drive west and south 84 miles until U.S. 101 reaches the coastal strip at Ruby Beach. A fifth is to drive west and south just over 100 miles on U.S. 101 to where the Queets Rain Forest Road branches northeast. And the sixth is to drive west and south about 120 miles on U.S. 101 to where the Quinault Rain Forest Road branches off near Amanda Park. From the latter, it is about 95 miles to I-5 at Olympia. Ferry service is also available from Victoria, British Columbia, across the Juan de Fuca Strait to Port Angeles.

By Air: Seattle-Tacoma International Airport (206-431-4444) is served by major airlines. Fairchild International Airport (360-457-8527) in Port Angeles is served by Horizon Air.

By Train: Amtrak (800-872-7245) stops in Seattle, Tacoma, and Olympia-Lacey.

By Bus: Greyhound Lines (800-231-2222) stops in Seattle. Gray Line of Seattle (800-426-

7532) offers summer bus tours of the Olympic Peninsula. Challam Transit (206-452-4511) offers commuter service Monday through Saturday from several locations and weekend trips to Hurricane Ridge in winter.

By Ferry: Washington State Ferries (800-84-FERRY or 206-464-6400) provides service across Puget Sound from Seattle, and Black Ball Transport (360-457-4491) offers ferry service between Port Angeles and Victoria, British Columbia.

Fees and Permits

Entrance fees are $10 per vehicle and $5 per person on foot, motorcycle, or by bus; passes are valid for seven consecutive days. Free backcountry camping permits are required and can be obtained at ranger stations and most trailheads. Fishing does not require a license, but a Washington State special punch card is required when fishing for steelhead and salmon.

Visitor and Information Centers

Olympic National Park Visitor Center, at 3002 Mt. Angeles Road: open daily year-round. Interpretive exhibits, programs, publications, maps, and backcountry permits.

Hurricane Ridge Visitor Center: open daily year-round, except when closed because of weather. Interpretive exhibits, programs, publications, and maps.

Storm King Information Center, on the shore of Crescent Lake: open daily in summer. Information.

Hoh Rain Forest Visitor Center: open daily year-round. Interpretive exhibits, publications, maps, and backcountry permits.

Kalaloch Information Station, near the southern end of the Pacific coastal strip: open daily only in summer.

Ranger stations are also located at Mora and Ozette on the coastal strip; Quinault Rain Forest, North Fork (summer), and Graves Creek (summer); Eagle (summer) near Sol Duc Hot Springs; Elwah; Heart O' the Hills (summer) south of Port Angeles; and Deer Park (summer), Dosewallips (summer), and Staircase, along the east side of the park.

Facilities

Lodging, restaurants, general stores, service stations, camping and fishing supplies, and ski and snowshoe rentals.

Handicapped Accessibility

The visitor centers, Hoh Mini-Trail, Madison Falls Trail, Kalaloch Lodge, restrooms at Dosewallips, Elwha, Fairholm, Graves Creek, Heart the Hills, Hoh, Kalaloch, Mora, Queets, Sol Duc, and Staircase campgrounds, and restrooms at Kalaloch and Mora group campgrounds are wheelchair accessible. A guide to Hurricane Ridge is available on cassette tape, and its subalpine meadows are accessible, with assistance, on several paved paths. For further information, call 360-452-0330.

Medical Services

First aid is available at park headquarters, visitor centers, and ranger stations. Hospitals are available in Port Angeles, Bremerton, Forks, and Aberdeen.

Pets

Pets are allowed on leashes not to exceed six feet in length. They are prohibited on trails, in the backcountry, and in some other areas as indicated by signs. Kennel facilities are available in Port Angeles.

Safety and Regulations

For your safety and enjoyment and for the protection of the park, please follow these regulations and suggestions:

- Stoves are recommended throughout the park and are required above 3,500 feet on the west side of the Elwha and North Fork of the Quinault and above 4,000 feet on the east side. Build fires below the timberline and in established fire rings.

- On beaches along the coastal strip, visitors should be alert for hazardous driftwood in the ocean waves and avoid the risk of hiking the headlands during incoming tides. The National Park Service advises obtaining a copy of the "Olympic Coastal Strip" folder at a visitor center or ranger station before hiking the coast.

- Before hikers set out on mountain treks, they should contact the National Park Service for up-to-date information on weather and trail conditions. As weather conditions can change quickly, it is always wise to be prepared with appropriate clothing and supplies.

- Feeding, disturbing, capturing, or hunting wildlife and damaging plantlife are prohibited.

The National Park Service asks that visitors not litter the park. Remember the excellent slogan to "leave only footprints" as a guide to help protect this national park.

ACTIVITIES

Hiking, mountain climbing, horseback riding, birdwatching, interpretive and educational programs, bicycling, picnicking, camping, boating (rentals are available), canoeing, kayaking, sailing, boardsailing, waterskiing, river rafting, swimming, fishing, cross-country and alpine skiing, and snowshoeing. Further information is available in the park's newspaper, *The Bugler*.

Hiking Trails

Among the 600 miles of trails are the following:

In the Hurricane Ridge Road vicinity:
Heart of the Forest Trail, a fairly easy, two-mile route through dense lowland forest, beginning at the Heart 'O the Hills Campground; **Hurricane Hill Trail**, a fairly easy, 1.5-mile route beginning at the end of Hurricane Ridge Road, proceeding through subalpine meadows filled with wildflowers in early summer, and providing views of the Olympic Mountains and the Strait of Juan de Fuca; and **Meadow Loop Trails**, a variety of routes beginning at the Hurricane Ridge Visitor Center and leading through subalpine meadows filled with wildflowers in early summer. A trail continues on to Klahhane Ridge.

In the Lake Crescent vicinity:
Moments in Time Nature Trail, an easy half-mile loop beginning near Lake Crescent Lodge, winding through beautiful old-growth forest, and providing views of Lake Crescent; **Marymere Falls Trail**, an easy one-mile

route beginning at Lake Crescent and leading through lush, old-growth forest to this beautiful, 90-foot waterfall; and **Mount Storm King Trail**, a fairly strenuous, 1.7-mile climb beginning at Marymere Falls and providing a ridgetop view of Lake Crescent. Hiking beyond this point is not recommended, except for persons with excellent route-finding and climbing skills.

In the Sol Duc River vicinity: **Sol Duc Falls Trail**, an easy .8-mile route beginning at the end of Sol Duc Road and winding through dense forest to this beautiful waterfall; **Mink Lake Trail**, a fairly strenuous, 2.5-mile, 1,400-foot climb beginning at Sol Duc Resort and ascending through dense forest to this beautiful lake; **Deer Lake Trail**, a fairly strenuous, 2.9-mile, 1,700-foot climb beginning at the Sol Duc trailhead on Sol Duc Road; and **Seven Lakes Basin Loop Trail**, a popular, strenuous, 18-mile route (a two- to three-day trek), beginning and ending at the Seven Lakes Basin trailhead on Sol Duc Road and looping around this glacier-carved basin that contains eight jewel-like lakes set amid subalpine meadows picturesquely dotted with subalpine firs and mountain hemlocks.

In the rainforest valleys: **Hoh Mini-Trail**, a very easy, quarter-mile, paved path through the lush rainforest; **Hall of Mosses Trail**, an easy, three-quarter-mile, self-guided interpretive walk beginning at the Hoh Visitor Center at the end of the Hoh Road and leading through the lush Hoh River valley rainforest; **Spruce Nature Trail**, an easy, 1.3-mile self-guided interpretive route, beginning at the Hoh Visitor Center; **Hoh River Trail**: a moderate, 11-mile route, beginning at the end of the Hoh Road and following the Hoh River through this spectacularly lush rainforest. Beyond this stretch, the trail climbs more steeply, following Glacier Creek up to Elk Lake, at just over 15 miles from the trailhead; to Glacier Meadows, at 17.3 miles from the trailhead; and ends on a stretch of primitive trail at Blue Glacier moraine, for a total distance of nearly 18 miles from the trailhead. For experienced mountaineers, the steep, hazardous, four-mile, 3,500-foot climb from Glacier Meadows is the shortest way to the summit of Mount Olympus; **Sams River Loop Trail**, an easy, three-mile route through the lush Queets River valley rainforest, beginning and ending a mile east of the Queets Ranger Station; **Maple Glade Rain Forest Trail**, an easy half-mile, self-guided interpretive loop walk through the lush Quinault River valley rainforest, beginning across the bridge from Quinault Ranger Station; and **Graves Creek Nature Trail**, an easy one-mile, self-guided interpretive loop through the lush Quinault River valley rainforest, beginning at Graves Creek Campground.

Along the Pacific coastal strip: **Cape Alava Trail**, an easy 3.3-mile, mostly boardwalk route to the westernmost point in the contiguous United States, beginning at the end of the Lake Ozette road. A 9.3-mile, nearly level loop hike includes this trail, three miles along the beautiful beach, and the Sand Point Trail. A current tide chart and weather conditions are posted at the trailhead; **Sand Point Trail**, an easy three-mile, mostly boardwalk route beginning at the end of the Lake Ozette road; **Rialto Beach Trail**, an easy .1-mile paved route beginning at the end of Mora Road and providing views of this beach, Cake Rock, and James Island; **Third Beach Trail**, an easy .8-mile route beginning at the La Push Road and providing views of seastacks and tidepools; and **Ruby Beach Trail**, a short walk from U.S. Route 101, providing views of this beach, seastacks, and Abbey Island. Six other short trails lead onto beautiful beaches to the south of Ruby Beach, providing opportunities to view tidepools and coastal scenery.

OVERNIGHT STAYS

Lodging and Dining

Visitors are advised to make reservations well in advance for the following facilities:

Lake Crescent Lodge, on Barnes Point, on the south shore of Lake Crescent, dating from 1916, open from late April to the end of October. Lodge rooms (without private bath), motel-type rooms, cabins, dining room, cocktail lounge, gift shop, and rowboat rental. HC 62, Box 11, Port Angeles, WA 98362; 360-928-3211.

Log Cabin Resort, at the northeast end of Lake Crescent, open from May to October. A-frame and rustic cabins, motel-type rooms, dining room, gift shop, grocery store, boat rental, boat launch, and an RV campground. 3183 E. Beach Road, Port Angeles, WA 98363; 360-928-3325.

Sol Duc Hot Springs Resort, dating from 1910 and renovated in 1988, open from mid-May to late-September. Simply furnished cabins, dining room, snack bar, swimming pool, three hot springs pools, gift shop, and grocery store. P.O. Box 2169, Port Angeles, WA 98362; 360-327-3583.

Kalaloch Lodge, at Kalaloch, just inside the southern end of the park's Pacific coastal strip, open year-round. Lodge and motel rooms, rustic cabins, restaurant, cocktail lounge, gift shop, grocery store, service station, guided tours, and interpretive programs. HC 80, Box 1100, Forks, WA 98331; 360-962-2271.

Lodging Outside the Park

Accommodations are available in nearby communities such as Port Angeles, Sequim, and Forks. Lake Quinault Lodge, dating from 1926, located just outside the park on Lake Quinault's South Shore Road in the Olympic National Forest, is open year round, providing simply furnished lodge and lakeside rooms, dining room, cocktail lounge, gift shop, indoor pool, sauna, jacuzzi, game room, and seasonal boat rentals; Box 7, Quinault, WA 98575; 800-562-6672 or 360-288-2900.

Campgrounds

All campgrounds operate on a first-come, first-served basis and have a 14-day limit-of-stay; some campgrounds close in the winter. Campgrounds may be closed because of snow. Reservations for group camping are required and can be made through the appropriate ranger stations.

Quotas are in effect from Memorial Day through Labor Day for the following. At Lake Constance and Flapjack Lakes, the daily limits are 20 people for Lake Constance and 30 for Flapjack Lakes. Camp permits can be acquired at the Dosewallips and Staircase ranger stations or reserved by calling 360-877-5569. At Ozette Loop Trail, a limited number of permits

are available for overnight camping on the Ozette Loop. Reservations are required and may be made by calling 360-452-0300.

Camping in the Seven Lakes Basin is limited to designated sites only. Permits must be obtained at Eagle (formerly Soleduck) ranger station, on a first-come, first-served basis.

Backcountry Camping

Permits are required for camping in the backcountry. When available, camp in a designated site; if not, choose sites at least a half mile from trailheads and 100 feet from lakes and streams. Campers should avoid areas marked for environmental restoration, and should camp on beaches safely above the high-tide line rather than in forests when on the coast. Water must be treated or should be packed in.

FLORA AND FAUNA (Partial Listings)

Mammals: Roosevelt elk, Columbian blacktail (mule) deer, black bear, mountain lion, bobcat, coyote, fisher, pine marten, Olympic shorttail weasel, river and sea otter, beaver, muskrat, mountain beaver, Olympic marmot, raccoon, spotted skunk, snowshoe hare, chickaree, Olympic and Townsend chipmunks, seals (harbor, elephant, and northern fur), northern (Steller) and California sea lions, Pacific white-sided dolphin, killer whale (orca), pilot whale (short-finned blackfish), harbor porpoise, and gray whale. Mountain goats, which were introduced into the Olympic Mountains in the 1920s, have caused a serious management problem in the park.

Birds: loons (red-throated, Pacific, and common), horned and eared grebes, cormorants (double-crested, Brandt's, and pelagic), common murre, tufted puffin, pigeon guillemot, marbled murrelet, Canada goose, mallard, wood duck, shoveler, green-winged teal, white-winged and surf scoters, harlequin duck, common and hooded mergansers, sooty shearwater, gulls (western, ring-billed, mew, glaucous-winged, and glaucous), black-legged kittiwake, black oystercatcher, semipalmated plover, killdeer, common snipe, spotted sandpiper, dunlin, sanderling, surfbird, black turnstone,

▲ Ruby Beach at low tide in Olympic National Park, Washington

great blue heron, ruffed and blue grouse, red-tailed hawk, bald and golden eagles, osprey, owls (great horned, spotted, and northern-pygmy), belted kingfisher, band-tailed pigeon, Anna's and rufous hummingbirds, woodpeckers (pileated, downy, and hairy), flicker, red-breasted sapsucker, flycatchers (olive-sided, willow, Hammond's, and Pacific-slope or western), horned lark, American pipit, Vaux's and black swifts, swallows (tree, northern rough-winged, violet-green, and barn), northwestern crow, raven, Steller's and gray jays, black-capped and chestnut-backed chickadees, bushtit, red-breasted nuthatch, brown creeper, wrens (winter, Bewick's, and marsh), dipper, golden-crowned kinglet, robin, Townsend's solitaire, thrushes (varied, Swainson's, and hermit), western bluebird, cedar waxwing, vireos (solitary, Hutton's, and warbling), warblers (yellow-rumped, Townsend's, hermit, black-throated gray, yellow, orange-crowned, yellowthroat, and Wilson's), red-winged blackbird, western tanager, sparrows (white-crowned, golden-crowned, fox, song, vesper, and savannah), rufous-sided towhee, dark-eyed junco, gray-crowned rosy finch, black-headed and evening grosbeaks, red crossbill, house and purple finches, and pine siskin.

Amphibians and Reptiles: salamanders (Cope's giant, northwestern, Olympic torrent, Ensatina, Van Dyke's, western red-backed, and long-toed), rough-skinned newt, western fence and northern alligator lizards, Cascades and northern red-legged frogs, Pacific tree frog, bullfrog, western toad, rubber boa, gopher snake, and garter snakes (common, western terrestrial, and northwestern).

Intertidal Organisms: brittlestar, stars (blood, rose, and sun), sea stars (ochre, pink, vermillion, and six-rayed), sea urchins (red, green, and purple), green and giant green sea anemones, checkered and Sitka periwinkles, chitons (lined, giant, mossy, hairy, and black), limpets (finger, speckled, shield, plate, duncecap, and keyhole), California and blue mussels, crabs (hermit, hairy, helmet, and turtle), goose and thatched acorn barnacles, piddock and razor clams, ringed topshell, channeled rock whelk, two-spot octopus, pink hydrocoral, sea hair, sea moss, sea lettuce, rockweed, surfweed, sea palm, sea cauliflower, sea sac, sea cabbage, split and bull kelp, red laver, rainbow seaweed, and coralline algae.

Trees, Shrubs, Flowers, and Ferns: western white and lodgepole pines, Sitka spruce, western and mountain hemlocks, firs (Douglas, grand or lowland, silver, and subalpine), western redcedar, Alaska (yellow) cedar, Pacific yew, Sitka and red alders, black cottonwood, willow, Pacific madrone, Pacific dogwood, cascara buckthorn, maples (bigleaf, western mountain, and vine), rhododendron, mountain heather, huckleberry, trailing blackberry, skunk cabbage, beargrass, cow parsnip, lilies (avalanche, glacier, Columbia tiger, and lambs-tongue), larkspur, painted-cups, magenta paintbrush, silky phacelia, spreading phlox, Lyall lupine, Calypso orchid, goatsbeard, pink and yellow monkeyflowers, oxalis, Piper bellflower, stonecrop, trillium, bunchberry, pink-flowered Flett violet, western pasqueflower, wallflower, woodland pinedrop, vanilla leaf, elephant's head, bracken, and ferns (deer, sword, maidenhair, and licorice).

NEARBY POINTS OF INTEREST

The areas surrounding Olympic National Park offer other exciting natural and historical attractions that can be enjoyed as day trips or overnight excursions. Olympic National Forest adjoins the park. Dungeness National Wildlife Refuge encompasses a narrow point of the Olympic Peninsula, extending into the Strait of Juan de Fuca. Ebey's Landing National Historical Reserve and San Juan Island National Historical Park are to the northeast in Puget Sound. North Cascades National Park and Ross Lake and Lake Chelan national recreation areas are to the northeast. Nisqually National Wildlife Refuge at the mouth of the Nisqually River in Puget Sound, Mount Rainier National Park, and the U.S. Forest Service-managed Mount St. Helens National Volcanic Monument are to the southeast. The Olympic Coast National Marine Sanctuary adjoins the park's Pacific coastal strip to the west.

OTHER NATIONAL PARK UNITS IN THE PACIFIC NORTHWEST REGION

▲ Sagebrush and the Painted Hills at John Day Fossil Beds National Monument, Oregon

Other National Park Units in the Pacific Northwest Region

City of Rocks National Reserve

P.O. Box 169
Almo, ID 83312
208-824-5519

This 14,407-acre national reserve in southern Idaho protects a scenic area of geologically spectacular spires, monoliths, columns, and other weather-sculpted, granite rock formations that were a prominent landmark for mid-19th-century pioneers and subsequently for the Utah-to-Idaho stage route. Some of the travelers, following the historic California Trail, wrote messages and other inscriptions on the rocks with axle grease. One pioneer wrote of these huge formations: "They are in a romantic valley clustered together, which gives them the appearance of a city." In 1852 alone, 52,000 people passed through the City of Rocks on their way to the California gold fields.

With elevations in the reserve ranging from 5,500 to 8,867 feet, visitor activities include hiking, technical rock climbing, bird-watching, picnicking, camping at designated primitive campsites, cross-country skiing, and snowshoeing. Backcountry permits, available at headquarters in Almo, are required for overnight excursions. A visitor center provides interpretive information, as well as rock-climbing regulations and the latest conditions of the reserve's unpaved roads.

Mammals in the reserve include mule deer, mountain lion, bobcat, coyote, red fox, badger, porcupine, spotted and striped skunks, jackrabbits, cottontails, whitetail antelope, golden-mantled and ground squirrels,

and chipmunks. Birds include the sage grouse, red-tailed and rough-legged hawks, golden eagle, bald eagle (in the winter), prairie falcon, great horned owl, mourning dove, black-chinned hummingbird, flicker, red-naped sapsucker, white-throated swift, violet-green swallows, raven, scrub and pinyon jays, black-billed magpie, mountain and black-capped chickadees, rock and canyon wrens, sage thrasher, robin, Townsend's solitaire, mountain bluebird, warblers (yellow-rumped, yellow, and orange-crowned), western tanager, sparrows (chipping, Brewer's, song, and vesper), rufous-sided and green-tailed towhees, black-headed grosbeak, lazuli bunting, Cassin's finch, and American goldfinch. Reptiles include striped whipsnake, gopher snake, and western rattlesnake, and lizards (sagebrush, desert horned, short-horned, and whiptail).

Among the reserve's nearly 550 identified species of vegetation are pines (limber, singleleaf pinyon, and lodgepole), Douglas fir, Utah juniper, western cedar, black cottonwood, quaking aspen, willows, mountain alder, mountain mahogany, red-osier dogwood, rabbitbrush, big sagebrush, currant, arrowleaf balsamroot, paintbrush, desert marigold, Rocky Mountain iris, lupine, penstemons, gilia, buckwheats, bluebell, violet, stonecrop, sagebrush buttercup, yellow bells, death camas, western peony, and prickly pear cactus.

The reserve, which is jointly managed by the National Park Service and the Idaho Department of Parks and Recreation, was authorized in 1988. Access is 56 miles from the Declo exit on I-84 to the reserve entrance: Drive south on State Route 77 through Albion, Elba, and two miles south of Almo. Then take the entrance road that branches to the west.

Craters of the Moon National Monument

P.O. Box 29
Arco, ID 83213
208-527-3257

This weird, moonscape-like national monument in southern Idaho protects 53,440 acres of an expanse of black volcanic craters, lava flows, lava tubes, and other features of once hot molten magma and violent explosions. Geologists believe the most recent of these outpourings from within the earth occurred between 15,000 and 2,000 years ago. The monument's roads, including the seven-mile Craters Loop Drive, provide excellent views of these prehistoric volcanic features. Among the hiking trails from which visitors can explore this fascinating environment are: the easy, quarter-mile North Crater Flow Trail; the easy, half-mile Devil's Orchard Nature Trail (which is also wheelchair accessible); the moderate, half-mile, paved Big Craters from the Spatter Cones Trail; the strenuous, but very scenic, half-mile Inferno Cone Trail; and the moderate, one-to-two-mile Caves Trail, leading a half-mile to Indian Tunnel and on to several other lava tubes. The National Park Service urges visitors to wear hiking boots or sturdy shoes and, especially in summer, to carry sufficient water and wear a hat and sunscreen as the heat of the sun is intense on the black lava.

Along with hiking and interpretive walks, visitor activities include birdwatching, picnicking, camping, and cross-country skiing. A visitor center provides interpretive exhibits, a video, and publications, and a campground is available nearby. Permits, available at the visitor center, are required for backcountry excursions.

The mammals of Craters of the Moon include mule deer, pronghorn, bobcat, coyote, red fox, badger, yellowbelly marmot, whitetail jackrabbit, pygmy rabbit, pika, golden-mantled and red squirrels, and yellow-pine chipmunk. Birds include sage grouse, prairie falcon, great horned owl, mourning dove, rufous hummingbird, flicker, violet-green swallow, raven, Clark's nutcracker, black-billed magpie, black-capped and mountain chickadees, rock wren, ruby-crowned kinglet, sage thrasher, robin, mountain bluebird, yellow-rumped warbler, Brewer's blackbird, western tanager, Brewer's sparrow, rufous-sided and green-tailed towhees, dark-eyed junco, lazuli bunting, Cassin's finch, and pine siskin. More than 300 varieties of plantlife have been identified; among them are limber pine, rabbitbrush, antelope bitterbrush, big sagebrush, tansybush, dwarf buckwheat, wire lettuce, bit-

terroot, scabland penstemon, syringa, Indian paintbrush, Anderson larkspur, blazingstar, cryptantha, arrowleaf balsamroot, dwarf monkeyflower, and prickly pear cactus.

To reach the monument, take the main highway between Arco and Carey (U.S. Routes 20/26/93), which goes directly through the area.

Hagerman Fossil Beds National Monument

**P.O. Box 570
Hagerman, ID 83332
208-837-4793**

This 4,345-acre national monument in southwest Idaho protects outstanding fossils embedded in the bluffs above the Snake River. The site is most important for 150 specimens of a small, long-extinct form of horse—the Hagerman horse, which inhabited this region around three million years ago. Other fossils include those of sabre-toothed cats, beavers, otters, birds, and fish. No visitor facilities presently exist at the site, but a visitor center is located in the town of Hagerman. Plans call for continuing paleontological research and for the display and interpretation of fossil specimens.

Nez Perce National Historical Park

**P.O. Box 93
Spalding, ID 83551
208-843-2261**

This 2,122-acre national historical park consisting of 38 scattered sites in Idaho, Washington, Oregon, and Montana commemorates the history, legends, and culture of the Nez Perce Indians, as well as their interaction with explorers, fur traders, Christian missionaries, U.S. soldiers, miners, and farmers who traveled through or settled in this region. Established in 1965, the park promotes an understanding and appreciation of Nez Perce people and helps keep alive their rich and diverse culture. Four sites in Idaho that are under the care of the National Park Service are **Heart of the Monster**, interpreting the Nez Perce creation legend (located between

Kamiah and Kooskia, on U.S. Route 12); **Canoe Camp**, where the Lewis and Clark Expedition paused and built canoes in 1805, before the final leg of their long trek to the Pacific coast (located 2.5 miles west of Orofino, on U.S. Route 121); **Spalding Mission**, where a Christian mission station was founded in 1836 (located 11 miles east of Lewiston, on U.S. Route 95); and **White Bird Battlefield**, site of the first official battle, in 1877, of the Nez Perce War (located in White Bird Canyon, about 14 miles south of Grangeville, on U.S. Route 95).

The **Bear Paw Battleground**, in northern Montana, is managed by the National Park Service, under an agreement with the state. Other sites are under various combinations of federal, state, tribal, and private ownerships. The park's visitor center, providing interpretive exhibits, programs, tours, walks, publications, and maps, is located at the Spalding site. (See also the entry on Big Hole National Battlefield.)

MONTANA

Big Hole National Battlefield

P.O. Box 237
Wisdom, MT 59761
406-689-3155

This 655-acre national battlefield in the Big Hole Valley of southwestern Montana memorializes the Nez Perce men, women, and children, soldiers of the U.S. Army, and civilian volunteers who clashed violently at the Battle of Big Hole in 1877. This conflict, a part of the larger Nez Perce War, produced an overwhelming loss of life and became the turning point in the long struggle by the U.S. military to confine the Nez Perce (and other Native Americans) to reservations. The battlefield's visitor center provides interpretive exhibits, an audiovisual program, and publications. During summer months, interpreter-led tours are offered. Self-guided tours on park trails are available year-round. The battlefield is open daily, except for Thanksgiving, Christmas Day, and New Year's Day. Among the access routes, visitors can take the I-15

Divide exit and drive west 61 miles on State Route 43. (See also the entry on the Nez Perce National Historical Park.)

Bighorn Canyon National Recreation Area

P.O. Box 7458
Fort Smith, MT 59035
406-666-2412

This 120,296-acre national recreation area in southern Montana and northern Wyoming encompasses 71-mile-long Bighorn Lake, created by Yellowtail Dam on the Bighorn River. Fifty-five miles of the reservoir lie within scenic Bighorn Canyon. Visitor activities include boating, waterskiing, swimming, fishing, hiking, and birdwatching. Visitor centers, located at Lovell, Wyoming, and Fort Smith, Montana, provide information and interpretive programs. Marinas, open from Memorial Day through Labor Day, are situated at both ends of the lake. To reach the recreation area: from I-90 at Hardin, Montana, drive south 44 miles on State Route 313 to Yellowtail Dam, at the north end; or from I-90, drive west 34 miles on U.S. Route 14 and then about 40 miles on U.S. Route 14A to the south end.

Grant-Kohrs Ranch National Historic Site

P.O. Box 790
Deer Lodge, MT 59722
406-846-3388

This 1,498-acre national historic site in the Deer Lodge Valley of western Montana commemorates the nation's frontier cattle era as it protects and interprets what was one of this country's largest and best-known 19th-century cattle ranches. Developed by Johnny Grant and later sold to Conrad Kohrs, this historic site illustrates the development of the Northern Plains cattle industry from the 1850s to recent times. Interpreter-led tours of the historic ranch house and self-guided walks around the complex are available. The visitor center provides interpretive exhibits and publications. As park staffing permits, living-history demonstrations are presented during the summer. The one-mile, self-guided, interpretive Cottonwood Creek Trail leads visitors through some of the ranch's natural environment, including riparian habitat. While picnicking and camping are not permitted on the ranch, facilities for both are located nearby. Grant-Kohrs Ranch is open daily, except on Thanksgiving, Christmas Day, and New Year's Day. Access to the site is from either of two Deer Lodge exits from I-90; the site is at the north end of town.

Little Bighorn Battlefield National Monument

P.O. Box 39
Crow Agency, MT 59022
406-638-2621

This two-unit, 765-acre national monument on the Crow Indian Reservation in southeast Montana memorializes one of the last armed efforts by the Northern Plains Indians in their attempt to preserve their ancestral way of life. Here, in the valley of the Little Bighorn River, on two days in June 1876, 263 soldiers and personnel of Lt. Col. George Armstrong Custer's battalion and others of the U.S. Seventh Cavalry were overwhelmed and killed by 1,500 to 2,000 Lakota, Cheyenne, and Arapaho warriors. Although the Indians won the battle, they subsequently lost the war against the country's effort to end their independent, nomadic way of life.

The national monument's visitor center provides interpretive exhibits, audiovisual programs, and publications. Guided bus tours and interpreter-guided walks are offered in the summer. Visitors walking the monument's trails during the summer months are cautioned to be alert for rattlesnakes.

Several trails lead to points of special interest, including Last Stand Hill where marble markers indicate where Custer's men perished. A granite monument marks the place where, in 1881, the bodies of enlisted men and others were placed in a mass grave. A memorial honoring the Indians who fought in this battle is expected to be erected soon. The monument is open daily, except on Thanksgiving, Christmas Day, and New Year's Day. To reach the national monument, take the U.S. Route 212 exit from I-90 and drive east one mile.

Fort Clatsop National Memorial

Route 3, Box 604-FC
Astoria, OR 97103
503-861-2471

This 125-acre national memorial in the northwest corner of Oregon protects the replica of Fort Clatsop, the fortified encampment occupied by Meriwether Lewis and William Clark's "Corps of Discovery" during the almost continuously wet and stormy winter of 1805-06. As defined by President Thomas Jefferson, the expedition's mission was to explore the Missouri River to its headwaters, cross over the Rocky Mountains, and proceed down the Columbia River to find the most direct route to the Pacific Ocean. The expedition through uncharted wilderness produced a wealth of detailed information on the geography, natural history, and Native Americans of the Great Plains and Pacific Northwest. It also awakened an interest among those living on the East Coast that soon lured a growing procession of explorers, trappers, and settlers into the region. Fort Clatsop itself consisted of a 50-foot-square fortified cabin compound in a thick coastal rainforest of Sitka spruce and western hemlock. It was named for the friendly Clatsop Indians who provided food and other vital assistance to the 45 men as they conducted environmental and cultural research and struggled through the long, miserable winter months.

A visitor center at the memorial provides interpretive exhibits, audiovisual programs, and publications, and living-history programs and exhibits are presented in the summer. Trails lead from the center to the fort and down to the historic canoe landing on the Lewis and Clark River. While a picnic area is available, camping is not permitted in the memorial. However, facilities are provided at nearby Fort Stevens State Park. Six miles of the Lewis and Clark Trail, from the fort to the Pacific Coast, are currently being constructed.

Mammals of the area include Roosevelt elk, blacktail (mule) deer, opossum, beaver, brush rabbit, western gray squirrel, chickaree, and Townsend chipmunk. Among the birds are mallard, pintail, wigeon, wood duck, green-winged and blue-winged teal, common merganser, great blue and green-backed herons, bald eagle, osprey, great horned owl, belted kingfisher, band-tailed pigeon, rufous hummingbird, woodpeckers (pileated, downy, and hairy), flicker, violet-green swallow, crow, raven, Steller's jay, black-capped and chestnut-backed chickadees, red-breasted nuthatch, wrens (winter, Bewick's, and marsh), kinglets, varied and Swainson's thrushes, Townsend's warbler, red-winged blackbird, white-crowned and golden-crowned sparrows, dark-eyed junco, black-headed grosbeak, and American goldfinch.

The lush vegetation includes Sitka spruce, Douglas fir, western hemlock, grand fir, western red cedar, red alder, willows, bigleaf and vine maples, salal, huckleberry, thimbleberry, elderberry, salmonberry, cascara buckhorn, Oregon grape, ferns (sword, deer, bracken, wood, and maidenhair), yellow iris, western trillium, wood sorrel, wood violet, fairybell, and touch-me-not.

To reach the memorial, drive south five miles from Astoria on U.S. Route 101 and Alt. 101.

John Day Fossil Beds National Monument

420 West Main Street
John Day, OR 97845-1031
503-987-2333

This 14,014-acre, three-unit national monument in the John Day Basin of north-central Oregon protects some of the world's richest paleontological records, with fossils of a tremendous diversity of flora and fauna that date from five to 45 million years ago. Paleontologists believe there is nowhere else in the world revealing a more complete sequence and continuity of Tertiary land plant and animal life. The national monument's Clarno unit protects the scenic Clarno Palisades, the fossils of hundreds of species of lush tropical and subtropical trees and other plantlife, and the fossils of mammals that inhabited this region between 35 and 45 million years ago, from some varieties that no longer exist to early forms of cat, tapir, and rhinoceros. The Painted Hills unit protects the fossils of more than 100

groups of mammals, including early forms of elephant, camel, horse, deer, bear, dog, cat, sloth, and rodent. The Sheep Rock unit contains the scenic Pictured Gorge and the monument's visitor center, which provides interpretive information and publications. All three units offer a number of short trails. While camping is not permitted, a picnic area is available in each unit.

Today's environment is more arid than that of the time span represented by the fossils. The variety of habitats include such animal species as mule deer, bobcat, coyote, badger, spotted and striped skunks, porcupine, raccoon, beaver, muskrat, blacktail jackrabbit, cottontail, Canada goose, cinnamon teal, common merganser, golden and bald eagles, California quail, belted kingfisher, Lewis's woodpecker, Steller's jay, black-billed magpie, rock and canyon wrens, mountain bluebird, Townsend's solitaire, yellow warbler, and red-winged and yellow-headed blackbirds. Of trees and other plantlife, there are ponderosa pine, western juniper, black cottonwood, willows, white alder, mountain mahogany, serviceberry, red-osier dogwood, sagebrush, rabbitbrush, shadscale, hopsage, greasewood, bitterbrush, snakeweed, purple sage, Indian paintbrush, penstemon, phacelila, goldaster, globemallow, wallflower, monkeyflower, blazingstar, pairie star, sunflower, and plains prickly pear and Simpson's hedgehog cacti.

To reach the monument's Clarno unit, take State Route 218 about 20 miles west of Fossil. To reach the Painted Hills unit, drive three miles west of Mitchell on U.S. Route 26 and then north six miles on an unnumbered road. To reach the Sheep Rock unit, drive six miles west of Dayville on U.S. Route 26 and then north on State Route 19.

Oregon Caves National Monument

19000 Caves Highway
Cave Junction, OR 97523
541-592-2100

This 487-acre national monument in the Siskiyou Mountains of southwestern Oregon protects a fascinating limestone cavern that features dripstone formations of calcite in narrow passageways. Above ground, the monument contains a lush old-growth forest. Among the flora and fauna are sugar pine, Douglas fir, western hemlock, Port Orford cedar, madrone, tan oak, rhododendron, ferns, black bear, blacktail (mule) deer, bobcat, gray fox, raccoon, chickaree, chipmunk, California and mountain quail, Lewis's woodpecker, Steller's jay, chestnut-backed chickadee, winter wren, varied thrush, and western tanager. Cave tours are available (visitors should wear warm clothing and soft-soled shoes), and trails wind through the monument. From Memorial Day through Labor Day, a monument concessionaire provides lodging and meals. Campground facilities are located four miles away in the surrounding national forest. To reach the monument from Grants Pass, Oregon, drive southwest 31 miles on U.S. Route 199 to Cave Junction, and east 20 miles on State Route 46. From Crescent City, California, drive northeast 54 miles to Cave Junction, and east 20 miles on Route 46.

WASHINGTON

Ebey's Landing National Historical Reserve

**P.O. Box 774
Coupeville, WA 98239
206-678-6084**

This 19,000-acre national historical reserve on Whidbey Island in Washington state's Puget Sound protects a rural district representing an unbroken record of exploration and settlement from the 19th century to the present. Historic farms, still under cultivation on the prairies of this island, continue land-use practices essentially unchanged since settlers claimed the land in the 1850s. Eight miles of beautiful beaches and bluffs extend along the shore. The seaport community of Coupeville, on the south shore of Penn Cove, contains many architecturally significant, Victorian-style homes, commercial buildings, and other historic structures.

Visitors may view much of the reserve's rural beauty by walking, bicycling, or driving on routes that lead to historic sites (including Admiralty Head Lighthouse), interpretive exhibits, and such scenic places as Rhododendron Park where flowers bloom in June. Brochures for self-guided tours are available at the Historical Museum. Trails lead hikers along the shore around Admiralty Head in Fort Casey State Park, at Ebey's Landing, and in Fort Ebey State Park. As more than 90 percent of the reserve is in private ownership, visitors are asked to be considerate of private property rights. Picnic and campsites are available in Fort Casey and Fort Ebey state parks and in Rhododendron Park.

To reach Whidbey Island from I-5 just north of Seattle, take State Route 525 and the ferry crossing from Mukilteo to Clinton. From I-5 at Burlington, drive west on State Route 20 or take the ferry crossing from Port Townsend on the Olympic Peninsula to Keystone.

Fort Vancouver National Historic Site

**612 East Reserve Street
Vancouver, WA 98661-3811
360-696-7655**

This 208-acre national historic site in southwest Washington state protects and interprets the land and reconstructed structures of the most significant 19th-century commercial center in the Pacific Northwest. From 1825 to 1849, Fort Vancouver was the western headquarters of the Hudson's Bay Company's fur-trading operations. The fort was originally established to generate profits and help secure Britain's claim to this region. However, as increasing numbers of American emigrants arrived in the Oregon country in the 1830s and 1840s, the fort provided supplies, extended credit, and even offered temporary lodgings that helped the new residents get established—thereby ultimately helping to bring the region into the United States.

From 1966 to 1982, the palisade and five buildings, including the Chief Factor's house and Indian Trade Shop, were reconstructed, and in 1995, the fur warehouse was completed. In 1996, Congress established the 366-acre **Vancouver National Historic Reserve**. This area includes Fort Vancouver, the adjacent city-owned Vancouver Barracks, a row of beautifully refurbished 19th century

U.S. Army residences, such as the O.O. Howard House and the Jack Murdock Aviation Center. The area recreates a pre-World War II airfield.

A visitor center provides interpretive exhibits, an audiovisual program, and publications. Interpretive tours are offered, and living-history demonstrations are presented. In July, special cultural events, such as the annual reenactment of the brigade encampment, are held at the fort. The site is open daily, except on Thanksgiving, Christmas Eve, and Christmas Day.

To reach the site, take the Mill Plain Blvd. exit from I-5, and drive east, following signs to the site on E. Evergreen Blvd. Alternatively, take the State Route 14 exit from I-205, and drive west about six miles to I-5 North to the Mill Plain Blvd. exit.

Klondike Gold Rush National Historical Park

117 South Main Street
Seattle, WA 98104
206-553-7220

All of this park—except a visitor center in the Pioneer Square Historic District of Seattle—is located in and near Skagway in southeast Alaska. The city of Seattle played a key role in one of the most spectacular gold rushes in North America, for it was here that word of gold in the Klondike first caught the imagination of the world and triggered a stampede of fortune hunters. And it was to this then-small port city that thousands of gold-seekers came on their way north to the Yukon. This visitor center provides interpretive exhibits, programs, and publications, as well as information on how to reach Skagway.

Lake Chelan National Recreation Area

2105 State Route 20
Sedro Woolley, WA 98284
360-856-5700

This 61,887-acre national recreation area on the east side of the Cascade Mountains of Washington state encompasses the lower part of ecologically rich Stehekin Valley and the upper five miles of Lake Chelan—a 55-mile-long natural lake in a glacially carved, long, narrow valley. With a depth of nearly 1,500 feet, Lake Chelan is the third deepest lake in the United States.

A visitor center in the valley provides interpretive exhibits and information, and interpreter-led walks and programs are offered from late June through early September. Other visitor activities include hiking, mountain climbing, horseback riding, birdwatching, boating, fishing, and hunting during the designated season. Hiking trails include the short, self-guided, interpretive Imus Creek Trail, scenic Lakeshore Trail, Agnes Gorge Trail, and the trail up to beautiful Rainbow Lake. A picnic area is located near spectacular, 312-foot Rainbow Falls, just off the unpaved, 20-mile road from Stehekin up to High Bridge and into North Cascades National Park. In addition to a number of campgrounds, lodging (for which reservations are usually needed far in advance) and meals are available in Stehekin.

Among the animals of the area are black bear, whitetail and mule deer, mountain lion, bobcat, coyote, red fox, porcupine, raccoon, striped skunk, pine marten, mink, weasel, chickaree, chipmunk, great horned and spotted owls, belted kingfisher, pileated woodpecker, Steller's and gray jays, Clark's nutcracker, raven, chickadee, red-breasted nuthatch, winter wren, kinglet, varied and hermit thrushes, robin, dipper, black-headed and evening grosbeaks, dark-eyed junco, white-crowned sparrow, western tanager, red crossbill, and rosy finch. Trees include ponderosa pine, western larch, Douglas fir, and bigleaf and vine maples.

Visitors to the area arrive by boat, with daily service from Chelan to Stehekin, from mid-March to the end of October; contact Lake Chelan Boat Company, Chelan, WA 98816; 509-682-2224. Visitors may also arrive by float plane; contact Chelan Airways, Chelan, WA 98816; 509-682-5555. From mid-May to mid-October, a daily shuttle service makes regular runs on the Stehekin Valley road. A fee is charged for the shuttle, and reservations are required; call 360-856-5700.

The recreation area's northwest end adjoins North Cascades National Park, so you may wish to also read the entries on North Cascades National Park and Ross Lake National Recreation Area.

Lake Roosevelt National Recreation Area

**1008 Crest Drive
Coulee Dam, WA 99116
509-633-9441**

Franklin D. Roosevelt Lake is the principal recreation feature of this 100,390-acre national recreation area in northeastern Washington state. The 130-mile-long reservoir created by Grand Coulee Dam offers opportunities for boating, waterskiing, swimming, fishing, hiking, camping, and tours of Fort Spokane and the dam. Boat rentals and boat ramps are available. The visitor center, located at the dam, is open daily, except on Thanksgiving, Christmas Day, and New Year's Day. A number of campgrounds are available along the lakeshore. During the summer, food services are provided at Seven Bay Marina and Spring Canyon Campground. Access to the recreation area from U.S. Route 2 to the dam is on State Route 155.

Ross Lake National Recreation Area

**2105 State Route 20
Sedro Woolley, WA 98284
206-856-5700**

This 117,574-acre national recreation area located between the northern and southern units of North Cascades National Park in northern Washington state offers many outdoor recreation opportunities.

Visitor activities include boating, canoeing, kayaking, and fishing in the mountain-framed reservoirs created by hydropower dams on the Skagit River. Also available are hiking, horseback riding, backcountry camping, interpreter-led walks, and several campgrounds. North Cascades Visitor Center provides interpretive exhibits and publications.

A number of trails lead hikers into the national park. Among other trails are two short self-guided interpretive routes from Newhalem Creek Campground called Trail of the Cedars

and To Know a Tree Trail. The Thunder Woods Nature Trail winds steeply from Thunder Creek Trail, near Colonial Campground, through an area of huge western red cedar trees. Big Beaver Trail is a popular route from Ross Lake Resort, along the shore of this lake. Reservations are recommended for lodging at Ross Lake Resort, Rockport, WA 98283; call 206-386-4437.

Among the animals of the recreation area are blacktail (mule) deer, black bear, mountain lion, bobcat, red fox, porcupine, raccoon, striped skunk, pine marten, mink, weasel, beaver, river otter, chickaree, chipmunk, bald eagle, great horned and spotted owls, belted kingfisher, pileated woodpecker, Steller's and gray jays, Clark's nutcracker, raven, chickadee, red-breasted nuthatch, winter wren, kinglet, varied and hermit thrushes, robin, dipper, dark-eyed junco, white-crowned sparrow, western tanager, red crossbill, and rosy finch. Trees include lodgepole pine, western hemlock, Douglas fir, western red cedar, and Pacific yew.

State Route 20 runs east-west through the recreation area, while the north end of Ross Lake is reached on an unpaved road that runs south from just west of Hope, British Columbia. Because of their proximity, see also the entries on North Cascades National Park and Lake Chelan National Recreation Area.

San Juan Island National Historical Park

**P.O. Box 429
Friday Harbor, WA 98250
360-378-2240**

This 1,752-acre national historical park in Puget Sound of northwest Washington state protects and interprets military sites of a lengthy 19th-century dispute between Britain and the United States over ownership of San Juan Island. In 1859, the deadlock over determining the location of the international boundary came close to a military confrontation when a U.S. farmer killed a British hog that had trespassed into his garden. As tensions quickly mounted, a company of U.S. troops was dispatched to the island, while a small fleet of British warships anchored offshore.

Fortunately, the "Pig War," as the event came to be called, did not lead to conflict, and the dispute was submitted to international arbitration. While awaiting the ruling, U.S. Army infantry were stationed at one end of the island and British marines at the other. In 1872, the arbitrator, Germany's Kaiser Wilhelm I, ruled that San Juan Island belonged to the United States.

The two-unit park protects the remains of earthworks and quarters of the U.S. encampment at the southern end of the island and the restored British barracks, guardhouse, and other structures at the north end. Visitor centers are located at Friday Harbor and American Camp; from mid-November through April, these centers are closed on national holidays. An additional visitor center, at English Camp, is open only in summer. Interpretive exhibits, programs, historical reenactments, and walks are provided, and trails and picnic areas are available. Access to the park is by Washington state ferry service from Anacortes, Washington, and from Sidney, British Columbia.

Whitman Mission National Historic Site

Route 2, Box 247
Walla Walla, WA 99362-9699
509-522-6360

This 98-acre national historic site in the Walla Walla River Valley of southeast Washington state protects and interprets the site of a Christian missionary station founded in 1836 by Marcus and Narcissa Whitman. The mission was established in an attempt to convert the Cayuse Indians at Waiilatpu (the "place of the people of the rye grass") to Christianity. It also served as an important emigrant house, providing lodging, food, and medical assistance for travelers on the Oregon Trail in the 1840s. While none of the mission buildings remains, a self-guided interpretive walk loops through the area where the main mission house, the emigrant house, and other structures once stood. A visitor center provides interpretive programs, exhibits, and publications. A picnic area is located near the center. To reach the site, drive seven miles west of Walla Walla on U.S. Route 12.

Continental Divide National Scenic Trail

U.S. Forest Service
P.O. Box 7669
Missoula, MT 59807
406-329-3150

This national scenic trail extends 3,200 miles from the Canadian to the Mexican border. So far, the longest designated stretch of this route extends nearly 800 miles from Glacier National Park in Montana to Yellowstone National Park in Wyoming. In addition to Glacier and Yellowstone, the trail runs through Rocky Mountain National Park in Colorado and several national forests. The trail runs adjacent to El Malpais National Monument in New Mexico.

Lewis and Clark National Historic Trail

National Park Service
700 Rayovac Drive, Suite 100
Madison, WI 53711
608-264-5610

This 3,700-mile trail extends from the Mississippi River in Illinois to the mouth of the Columbia River in Oregon and celebrates the epic Lewis and Clark Expedition of 1804-1806. Roads, trails, and rivers connect the route's historic sites, which are variously managed by federal, state, and local governmental agencies as well as private organizations. National Park Service units along the route are Jefferson National Expansion Memorial in St. Louis, Missouri; Knife River Indian Villages National Historic Site in North Dakota; Nez Perce National Historical Park in Montana, Idaho, Oregon, and Washington; Fort Vancouver National Historic Site in Washington State; and Fort Clatsop National Memorial in Oregon.

Nez Perce (Nee-Me-Poo) National Historic Trail

U.S. Forest Service, Region 1
P.O. Box 7669
Missoula, MT 59807
406-329-3582

This 1,170-mile national historic trail commemorates the flight in 1877 of the "nontreaty"

Nez Perce Indians, who for months attempted to outrun pursuing U.S. Army troops. The trail extends from northeastern Oregon through Big Hole National Battlefield in Idaho and Yellowstone National Park in Wyoming to near the Bear Paw Mountains in Montana.

Oregon National Historic Trail

Long Distance Trails Office
National Park Service
P.O. Box 45155
Salt Lake City, UT 84145-0155
801-539-4094

Extending 2,170 miles from Independence, Missouri, to Oregon City, Oregon, this historic route was used by fur traders, trappers, fron- tiersmen, gold-seekers, missionaries, and more than 300,000 emigrants from the 1840s through the 1850s. The trail is cooperatively managed by the National Park Service, U.S. Bureau of Land Management (BLM), U.S. Forest Service, state and local governmental agencies, and private organizations. Among the highlights are Scotts Bluff National Monument and Chimney Rock National Historic Site in Nebraska, Hagerman Fossil Beds National Monument in Idaho, and Whitman Mission and Fort Vancouver national historic sites in Washington state. Several Bureau of Land Management sites are also along the route, including Oregon National Historic Trail Corridor Sites in Wyoming; Bonneville Point Section of the Oregon Trail, which is seven miles east of Boise, Idaho; and National Historic Oregon Trail Interpretive Center, near Baker City, Oregon.

Pacific Crest National Scenic Trail

U.S. Forest Service
P.O. Box 3623
Portland, OR 97208
503-326-3644

This national scenic trail extends 2,638 miles from Canada to Mexico. It runs through North Cascades National Park and Lake Chelan National Recreation Area in Washington to Crater Lake National Park in Oregon. In California, the trail crosses Lassen Volcanic and Yosemite national parks, Devils Postpile National Monument, and Sequoia and Kings Canyon national parks.

FRIENDS OF THE PARKS ORGANIZATIONS

Craters of the Moon Project
P.O. Box 4715
Boise, ID 83711
208- 322-3422

Custer Battlefield Preservation Committee
(Little Bighorn Battlefield Nat'l Monument)
P.O. Box 7
Hardin, MT 59034
406-665-1876

Friends of Crater Lake National Park
P.O. Box 88
Crater Lake, OR 97604
541-594-2211, ext. 300

Friends of Fort Vancouver
c/o Ft. Vancouver Nat'l Historic Site
612 E. Reserve Street
Vancouver, WA 98661
360-695-7655, ext. 11

Friends of the San Juans
P.O. Box 1344
Friday Harbor, WA 98250
206-378-2319

Friends of the Elwha
(Olympic Nat'l Park)
122 E. 9th Street
Port Angeles, WA 98362
360-452-4072

Hagerman Fossil Council, Inc.
P.O. Box 56
Hagerman, ID 83332
208-543-8334

Lewis and Clark Trail Heritage Foundation, Inc.
P.O. Box 3434
Great Falls, MT 59403
406-453-7091

Mt. Rainier, North Cascades, and Olympic Fund
1221 2nd Avenue, Suite 350
Seattle, WA 98101
206-621-6565

Nez Perce National Historic Trail Foundation
P.O. Box 20197
Missoula, MT 59801
406-728-7649

North Cascades Conservation Council
P.O. Box 95980, Union Station
Seattle, WA 98145-1980
206-343-2312

Olympic Park Associates
13245 40th Avenue, NE
Seattle, WA 98105
206-364-3933

Olympic Park Institute
111 Barnes Point Road
Port Angeles, WA 98362
206-928-3720

Oregon-California Trails Association
P.O. Box 1019
Independence, MO 64051
816-252-2276

Pacific Crest Trail Conference
P.O. Box 2514
Lynnwood, WA 98036-2514

Cooperating Associations

Crater Lake Natural History Association
P.O. Box 157
Crater Lake, OR 97604
541-594-2211

Craters of the Moon Natural History Association
P.O. Box 29
Arco, ID 83213
208-527-3257

Fort Clatsop Historical Association
Route 3, Box 604-FC
Astoria, OR 97103
503-861-2471

Glacier Natural History Association
P.O. Box 428
West Glacier, MT 59936
406-888-5756

National Trust for Historic Preservation
1785 Massachusetts Avenue, NW
Washington, DC 20036
202-673-4000

Northwest Interpretive Association
909 First Avenue, Suite 630
Seattle, WA 98104
206-220-4140

Oregon Trail Museum Association
Scotts Bluff National Monument
P.O. Box 27
Gering, NE 69341
308-436-2975

Student Conservation Association
1800 N. Kent Street
Arlington, VA 22209
703-524-2441

L O C A L   C O L O R

The Wildlife

"Texas" means friend.

Texas was a country before it was a state.

25 languages.

65 nationalities.

Texans believe life is too important to be dull.

The Wildflowers

The state flower is the Bluebonnet.

Over 5,000 species of wildflowers.

There's even a Wildflower Center (Thanks to Lady Bird Johnson).

Texas does not have blue grass. It just seems that way.

It's like a whole other country.®

Even the vacations are bigger in Texas. From the yarn-spinning charm of our native citizenry to hills carpeted with our native flowers, you'll find it all in Texas. It's more than you think. It's like a whole other country. For your free Texas travel guide, you can visit our web site at 💻 **www.TravelTex.com** or call us at ☎ **1-800-8888-TEX (Ext. 1290).** So give us a call, y'all.

NPCA Checks
Save Our Parks!

Every order helps preserve our country's most precious areas. Every time you order, royalties go directly to the National Parks and Conservation Association.

Return Address Labels - six scenes match your checks!

Hemp Checkbook Cover features the NPCA logo

Cotton Covers- select your favorite scene

Acadia

Everglades

Yellowstone

Arches

Smoky Mountains

Yosemite

Beautiful rotating series features the Great Smoky Mountains, Yosemite, Arches, Yellowstone, Acadia, and Everglades National Parks.

IF WE DON'T PROTECT THEM, WHO WILL?

LEND YOUR VOICE TO HELP SAVE OUR CROWN JEWELS.

The national parks belong to you and me, and they are the most important, meaningful and irreplaceable resource we have to give to future generations.

Unfortunately, our parks are in crisis! Almost every single one of the 378 national park units is troubled by problems of overcrowding, pollution and destructive uses that threaten to permanently damage these precious places...but there is hope.

For 80 years the National Parks and Conservation Association has been the only private, nonprofit citizens' organization dedicated solely to preserving and protecting our National Park System. Over the years, some of our accomplishments have included: saving parks from toxic mining plans and nearby nuclear waste dumps, brokering pollution-abating air quality agreements, and working with Congress to implement concessions reform — that stopped businesses from profiting unfairly from the parks!

Our work is far from over and we need your help now! Please join National Parks and Conservation Association and lend your voice to the nearly 400,000 others who help us in our daily fight to save these parks. Thank you!